FORMING AGILE TEAMS
WORKBOOK

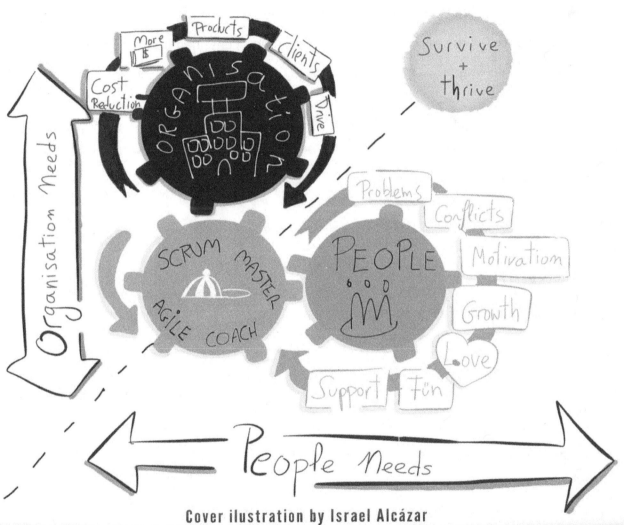

Cover ilustration by Israel Alcázar

Techniques for structuring and get sustainable Agile Teams high-performance ready

Jesus Mendez

Legal Deposit

Bibliothèque et Archives du Canada, 2016.

Bibliothèque et Archives nationales du Québec, 2016.

The author and the publisher have taken care in the preparation of this workbook but make no expressed or implied warranty of any kind and assume no responsibility for errors or omissions, or for changes that occur after publication. No liability is assumed for incidental or consequential damages in connection with or arising out of the use of the information or programs contained herein. Further, the author and the publisher have no responsibility for content on third-party websites.

The publisher offers discounts on this workbook when ordered in quantity for bulk purchases or special sales, which may include electronic versions and/or content particular to your business, training needs, marketing purposes, and branding interests.

For more information, please contact:

Jesus Mendez

(438) 883-3162

transformingteams@jesusmendez.ca

Publisher: Jesús E. Méndez A.

ISBN: 9781670489043

Book design: Jesus Mendez

Book illustration cover: Israel Alcázar

Edition: Natural Vision Inc.

Revision: #2, December 2019

About the Workbook

This workbook contains a set of tools and techniques to help Scrum Masters, Facilitators, Agile Coaches and Agile Practitioners when forming teams. It has been created mainly to share the artifacts and techniques that I've developed from what I've learned, the challenges that I've faced and how I've got through it when Forming teams.

The Author

Jesus is all about helping people with finding ways to reach their highest potential by offering the gift of coaching. He has contributed in delivering more than 20 projects over his combined professional career. A passionate reader, who has spent the last five (5) years observing, trying, documenting, experimenting and growing software development teams through different tools, games, activities and processes to help them walk through the stages of the group development theory proposed by Bruce W. Tuckman.

Table of Contents

Introduction

The tools provided in this workbook pretend to offer an alternative-proven path to help with adding more structure, transparency and visibility to what we do when assisting Agile teams, by combining visual explanations with techniques and tips to support our crucial role within the organization as Scrum Masters/Agile Coaches/Agile Leaders.

Inspired from what I have been doing during the past ten (10) years when forming agile teams, I have created on the top of the traditional Scrum framework, what I have called the "Forming Agile Teams Flow". A step by step flow, composed by nine (9) steps to facilitate understanding and give you a better idea about what, why, how and when I recommend using the techniques suggested in the text that you are about to read.

It's important for you to know that the techniques and tools that you'll find documented in this workbook, are the result of a practical journey, plenty of learning, try outs, a lot of reading, meeting and collaborating with beautiful and exceptional people, a lot of hours of introspection and self-growing.

My intention is to provide you with techniques to ease your journey and increase the impact that you have over your teams; a way to start over that could help you with helping your teams to get organized, structured and navigate towards the next stage of the Tuckman's theory of group development: "Storming".

I wish you all the best with reducing team's ambiguity by increasing clarity through an incredible and nurturing experience.

Forming teams

Bruce Wayne Tuckman Theory of group development
Forming, Storming, Norming, Performing, Adjourning

According to Bruce Tuckman's group development theory a team undergoes various stages with time in-order to perform with its 100% productivity level.

Tuckman, B., Jensen, M. 1997

Finish

Stage 5 Adjourning: Having completed their task the group dissolves. Members will share either a sense of loss or relief, depending on the outcome of the task.

Stage 4 Performing: Confidence grows both individually and with other members of the group as they work towards a common goal.

Stage 3 Norming: The group find ways of resolving conflict and begin to emerge as a cohesive unit. Criticisms and feedback are given constructively and members start co-operating with one another.

Stage 2 Storming: Conflict occurs as personal agendas come to light. Members assert themselves and start questioning decisions and challenging authority.

Stage 1 Forming: Members start interacting and try to work out what is expected of them. Excitement and enthusiasm is mixed with fear and uncertainty.

Development of team

Start

Figure 1- Tuckman's Theory of group development - Stages

Being curious and passionate about helping people and teams to thrive in a sustainable fashion had brought to me to think about the following question: how could I help agile teams navigate through each stage of Tuckman's model, in a practical way? What techniques should I use? What kind of challenges am I going to face? How do I do it?

Well, the best way that I knew by the time I've started writing this workbook and the best approach that I know so far is to do it by iterations.

This workbook describes a well-tested path to help Scrum Masters/Agile Coaches and Agile Practitioners navigate teams through the early stage of their development, more specifically those that are in the Stage 1: Forming of Tuckman's theory of group development model.

Let's start "Forming agile teams" by exploring some of the challenges that you'll face when doing it:

Forming Agile teams

Challenges

Everything that occurs with Tuckman's theory of group development forming stage will set the foundations for the team to go through its different stages. It's in this stage where:

- Stakeholders will be super anxious about how things are going to work and what's planned for the team in order to get results that will bring value as soon as possible.
- Some boundaries will be set in terms of the product or service that the future team will be delivering.
- Trust will be established between you and the team and between the team members as well.
- The team will discover who does what and what makes each team member different and special.
- The identity and team's purpose will be determined.
- The tone of every single conversation that will lead the team to succeed will be set.
- Your superpowers must be used to show the team what the path to sustainable high-performance looks likes.
- Your senses will be tested, and you'll use them to help you decide what to do, how to do it and when to do it.

Our role in the Team Transformation Process

As Scrum Masters/Agile Coaches we have a main role within the team's transformation process. In my opinion, we should be leading the change process collaborating with a team composed by at least one representative of each group who has an interest in the team to be transformed.

Further than that, I truly believe that installing common sense should be our MOTTO. Guide people, teams and organizations to understand that being agile means to use the common sense in every single circumstance. I also believe in the benefits of connecting people by collaborating, as our main mission as people's helpers. These could sound easy to do, but in practice it might be hard to get, especially when the only authority that you would have over people, comes from your ability to influence their lives and help them welcome change as make it part of their journey.

It's a big, to be leading by example and permanently be there to inspire others to inspect and adapt. It requires courage, self-awareness, humbleness, love and hope that the best will come if we do it together.

Well, that's our role in the team's transformation process. We are at heart of it, and yes, it's up to you to make the difference and change the world, one team at a time.

Techniques

Let's walk through the techniques that I've used to helping teams face the challenges mentioned above, and successfully navigate from the forming stage to the next stage of Tuckman's theory of group development "storming".

Forming agile teams flow

I'm a visual person, I need drawing to put ideas together and be able to learn, digest and then share my understandings with people. One day, I was having a hard time getting thoughts out of my head; I was stuck and frustrated because that something to connect all the dots was missing in the book. It was then when after talking about it with my friend **Ida Perciballi**[1], one of the Product Owners that I have the pleasure to work with, and after explaining her my frustration, where she proposed me this brilliant idea of creating a workflow to walk readers through the team transformation process and contextualize where to apply the techniques that I'm proposing in this workbook for forming agile teams.

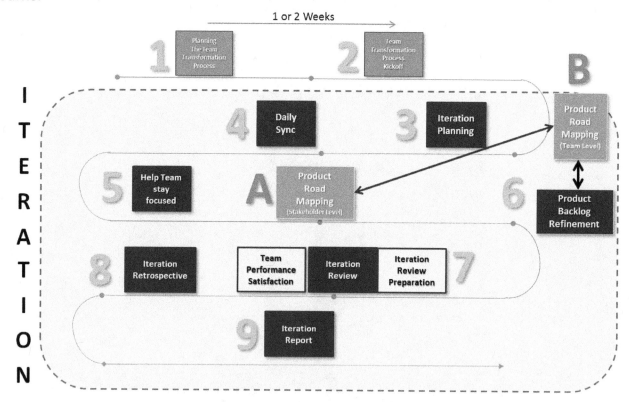

Figure 2- Forming Agile Teams Flow

---

[1] Ida Perciballi, Product Owner at Seedbox Technologies Inc., https://www.linkedin.com/in/idaperciballi

That's what I thought I was looking at; a way to explain the techniques that I've learned when forming agile teams by using a visual diagram to put all the ideas together and I came up with this diagram that I've called the "Forming Agile Teams Flow", inspired by a typical sprint as described in the Agile Scrum framework.

The "Forming Agile Teams Flow" has nine (9) steps and two (2) complementary events for product planning to add an additional dimension to facilitate connecting what the team is developing (technology) with what the company wants and needs (business).

The first two (2) steps (Planning the Team Transformation Process and Team Transformation Process Kick-off) refers to the preparation work that I think needs to be done before starting to form an agile team. The other seven (7) steps (Iteration Planning, Daily Sync, Help the Team stay focused, Product Backlog Refinement, Iteration Review Preparation, Iteration Review, Team Performance Satisfaction, Iteration Retrospective and Iteration Report) have been considered to be done within the iteration time frame established for the particular agile team that you are about to start forming.

It's all done by iterations

By definition, **iteration** refers to "the repetition of a process or utterance". The Agile Alliance guide defines iteration in the context of agile projects as "a time box during which development takes place, the duration of which:

- May vary from project to project, usually between 1 and 4 weeks.
- Is in most cases fixed for the duration of a given project."

Scrum.org defines sprints as "the heart of Scrum, a time-box of one month or less during which a "Done", useable, and potentially releasable product Increment is created".

Mike Cohn[2] mentions on his article **"Differences between Scrum and Extreme Programming"**[3] what follows: "Scrum teams typically work in iterations (called sprints) that are from two weeks to one month long. XP teams typically work in iterations that are one or two weeks long".

In the context of the workbook, when it refers to Iterations we are talking about a time-box of one week to a month during which a "Done" useable product that resolves a customer problem increment is built by the agile team.

What activities compose a typical iteration in the context of this workbook?

The following table lists the activities that compose a typical iteration in the context of this workbook:

Activity	Description
Iteration	During the **Iteration**, the development team collaborates to build what has been identified during the iteration planning. The development team cooperates with the Product Owner to develop what brings more value to the customers. Iterations are flexible, so small changes are allowed by swapping stories that the team hasn't worked on, with new stories already refined together. It's possible to remove content from the iteration and teams are encouraged to embrace change to listen to use feedback. Communication and collaboration facilitate changes and keeps everyone doing what makes more sense reducing waste as much as possible.

---

[2] Mike Cohn, https://www.mountaingoatsoftware.com/company/about-mike-cohn
[3] Mike Cohn, https://www.mountaingoatsoftware.com/blog/differences-between-scrum-and-extreme-programming

Activity	Description
Iteration Planning	The **Iteration planning** it's a cooperative and collaborative event that requires customer voice representative (The Product Owner), the development team and all specialists need it to make the iteration goal a reality. Because the Product Owner has the most information about value (after negotiation with the customer)—he/she is the most qualified to say what is important—he/she prioritizes." "Because the development team have the most information about costs—they're most qualified to say how long it will take to implement a story—they estimate" also because they are considered the experts.

Activity	Description
Iteration Daily Sync	The **Daily sync** is considered as the "event for the development team to synchronize activities and create a plan for the next 24 hours" within the Scrum guide provided by Scrum.org.

Activity	Description
Team's Road Mapping	The **Team's Road Mapping** is an event that happens once per quarter, were the Product Owner assisted by the Scrum Master/Agile Coach, would identify what goals would be reached by the team in the upcoming three months. Once that the first version is done, the Product Owner would collaborate with the Development team to get ready to tackle what's coming within the next Product Backlog Refinement session.

Activity	Description
Product Backlog Refinement	**Product Backlog refinement** allows the agile team to keep the product backlog updated for upcoming iterations. Product Backlog refinements happens at the same time and at the same place during the iteration, at least once. The Product Owner could call for an additional Product Backlog refinement when need it during the iteration, in order to validate the potential cost (estimate) of each user story. Product backlog refinements are held to enable discussion between the development team and the Product Owner and facilitate challenging what should be done and why would be done now.

Activity	Description
Iteration Review Dry Run	The **iteration review Dry-run** is the event where the agile team would prepare what would be delivered at the iteration review. It's 30 minutes to 1-hour meeting, for the development team to go through the iteration backlog in order to validate with the Product Owner, what has been done and what is left to be done. By using the Iteration Review Template, the Scrum Master/Agile Coach would help the team to organize the information to be shared at the

| | iteration review, like for example the iteration status, what would be demonstrated, what would be the list of updates (no demo include it), what's worthy to be shown event if is not 100% done and what's next in terms of the Product. |

Activity	Description
Iteration Review	The **iteration review** is the event where the development team shows the work that's completed within the iteration and that has been validated and approved by the Product Owner. It's also the time within the iteration to collaborate with stakeholders about the Product and get feedback about the work that the team has done.
	By the end of the Iteration review, it's time to evaluate the **team's performance satisfaction** regarding the work that the team has done during the iteration. By using The Team's Performance Satisfaction Template, stakeholders and the agile team would share their happiness level regarding the team's performance; by tagging their names into the face that reflects better their impression about the team.

Activity	Description
Iteration Retrospective	During the **Iteration retrospective**, the development team collaborates to develop what was identified during the iteration planning. The development team cooperates with the Product Owner to develop what brings more value to the customers. Iterations are flexible, so small changes are allowed by swapping stories that the team hasn't worked on, with new stories already refined together. It's possible to remove content from the iteration and teams are encouraged to embrace change to listen to use feedback. Communication and collaboration facilitate changes and keeps everyone doing what makes more sense reducing waste as much as possible.

Activity	Description
Iteration Reporting	By the end of the iteration, the Scrum Master/Agile Coach will create the **Iteration Report** by using the Iteration Report Template in order to increase visibility at the organization level about what the team has done during the iteration, raise risks and create awareness by being transparent.

Iterations: How long it last?

It really depends of the team. In my experience, two (2) weeks iteration is good enough for the development team to deliver high quality products and for the organization to keep participating on agile ceremonies.

> 💡 **Tip:** If the team identifies that the duration of their iteration is an impediment for them to complete what they have committed to do, then challenge them to look for the root cause of it. Usually what happen is that the team is over committing, or that a hidden issue is causing the team to ask for more time to finish what needs to be done.

In my experience, I like to suggest my teams to avoid changing the duration of the iteration, so then the agile team can develop consistency, create its own pace and set a rhythm.

Why iterations?

Some of the principles behind the **manifesto for agile software development**[4] justify the fact of having iterations to develop software:

"Deliver working software frequently, from a couple of weeks to a couple of months, with a preference to the shorter timescale"

"Agile processes promote sustainable development. The sponsors, developers, and users should be able to <u>maintain a constant pace indefinitely</u>"

"At regular intervals, the team reflects on how to become more effective, then tunes and adjusts its behavior accordingly"

From what I've seen in the field when forming agile teams, having iterations facilitates team learning by allowing repetition which set team habits in time and brings the required structure to shape teams growing.

---

[4] The Manifesto for Agile Software Development, www.agilemanifesto.org

1. Planning the team transformation process

Before meeting the team, there is a change to be managed, planned and communicated, and that's the change that you are about to begin when transforming the team into a high-performing sustainable team. A change that requires a lot of effort in time and money which, in my opinion, needs to be supported with a transition plan. But why do we need a plan to transform a team, isn't it something that's going to happen in an agile fashion, I mean iteration by iteration? Why should we care about planning changes, when playing the Scrum Master or Agile Coach role? Well in my personal opinion it depends, but I prefer to have a clear understanding about what's motivating the stakeholders to invest resources in what I've called "the team's transformation project".

At this stage of the project, there is not a lot of information about:

- The reasons behind hiring or even assigning a Scrum Master or Agile Coach to the team.
- Who does what, when and how things are going to happen (what's the plan?)
- The team and its composition.
- How the team works.

What's the main goal here?
"Mitigate change resistance by reducing ambiguity, increasing visibility and creating awareness about the project at every level involved"; in order to gain the people's trust and create the required conditions to successfully reach the people's heart.

How to do it? How to get everybody involved in the project and on the same page?
First of all, I gather enough information to create the "project charter", by talking with all the parties involved in the "team's transformation project". Here are the steps that I follow to complete this stage of the process:

Preliminary work (It's all about the team and the environment)

Purpose: Get ready to talk with project's main stakeholder.

Tactic: Collect information about the team by meeting with their line manager(s) and asking questions like:

- Is the team being formed for this specific project?

- How long the team has been working together?

- What about team's development process?
- Who are the main stakeholders of the project?
- Who are the customers?
- How does the teamwork?

 Tip: Try to understand how the team works first and then think with them, what to do next.

Project Charter content gathering meeting

Purpose: Collect enough information to get everybody on the same page and begin the project as soon as possible.

Tactic: meet with project main stakeholder(s) to answer a list of crucial questions for the project:
- What's the project about?
- Why are we doing this right now?
- Reason and strategy
- Who is doing what? Help with identifying roles and responsibilities.
- What are the biggest business and operational risks, associated to the project?
- What's your vision of the team a year from now?
- What are the top three main goals, for the short term (3 months ideally)?
- Is there any suggestion on how the process of the team's work should be conducted?

Outcome: The team's transformation process Project Charter information has been gathered.

Fill the Team's Transformation Process Project Charter template

Purpose: Document the shared understanding baseline of the project.

Tactic: Focus on documenting just enough information to describe what the project is about.

Outcome: Team's transformation Project Charter is completed and ready to be shared.

 Tip: Keep it simple and document no more than two (2) pages.

High level project plan approval meeting

Purpose: Get common agreement about what the project is about and get the project plan approved. Begin working with the team.

Tactic: Focus on documenting just enough information to describe what the project is about.

Outcome: Team's Transformation Process Project Charter has been approved.

Team's transformation project kick-off meeting

Purpose: Shared understanding for team project members about the team's transformation project.

Tactics: Hold a one-hour meeting and be sure that all interested parties are present. Ask the main project stakeholder to set the stage by sharing with the audience the two first components of the team's transformation project charter:

1. What's the project about?
2. Why are we doing it right now?
3. Reasons and the strategies to get it done.

Now, it is your turn to go through the remaining content of the team's transformation process project charter:

1. Roles and responsibilities
2. Vision of the team in one (1) year from now.
3. Short term main goals identified.
4. High level project risks.
5. Identify the next step in the plan

> **Tip:** Print out a copy of Team's transformation process project charter for every person present in the meeting.

2. Team transformation process Kick-off

Preparation
Once the Team's transformation project charter is approved, it's time to meet with your new team and start building the relationship of trust required to move forward with the transformation process.

What's the main Goal here?
Establish a relationship of trust between you and your team that would enable the path to the continuous improvement on-going conversation for the team.

Why is this priority?
If you consider yourself as a change agent, the main thing for people to start changing their mindsets is to trust the person who represents change. Having their trust means getting their hearts and believes in you and what you will bring to the team.

How to do it? How to establish a relationship of trust?

The focus here is to create the conditions and environment to make people feel safe enough to get out of their comfort zones and learn to change continuously.

Let's discuss about what needs to be taken into consideration at this stage:
- What's the team history?
- Who are the team sponsors?
- Who are the key people in the team?
- How is the team doing things?
- How to know that the relationship of trust has been established?

It's all about the people
Getting to know the people that you're about start working with requires time, love and strategy. In my case, I use the steps of **the arc of a coaching conversation[5]** to approach the team and start learning about them. The first thing that I do is "**start exploring**". Depending of the project, I give to myself a full iteration at least to explore and observe respectfully how the team behave, interact, collaborate and work together. During this period, I would try to identify:
- What type of team is this? Hierarchical, Breakthrough, Synchronized, Open.
- Who are the key people within the team? Identify their names.

---

[5] Sue Johnston, The Arc of a Coaching Conversation

- About people's collaboration: Does it exists? Yes or No
- About people's motivation: Is everybody motivated? Yes or No
- About people's interactions: What's the voice tone used between people in the team? Positive, Negative or Other Tones.

What's the main focus here?

Our main job here is to be present for the team and be ready to listen actively what and how it's being said. The intension here is to get enough contexts about the team so it's recommended to avoid judgement and put your ears up.

> **Tip:** Being outside of the group as an observer would show the team that you respect their space. Pay attention to where you place yourself. I used to putting myself out of the team area.

In order to help explore, I like using use "What" questions, combined with a polite approach, for example:

- About the recurrent meetings that the team have, would you mind telling me what 's the team's schedule?
- About the development process, what are the steps of the team's current development process?
- About the team, what does the team likes about working together?
- About the project, what are the project main goals?
- About the product/service, is there any product/service vision available? Do you mind sharing it with me?

The leadership team first

Some of the questions mentioned above, would be answered directly by the leadership team; I mean the Project Stakeholders, the Product/Service owner and the line manager(s). That's why I strongly recommend meeting with them first, in order to discuss about their vision regarding the project, the product or service and the team.

The leadership team would be supporting what we are about to do with the team, that's why it's really important to get them on board collaborating with us, to enable the change within the team, then with the project, and so on.

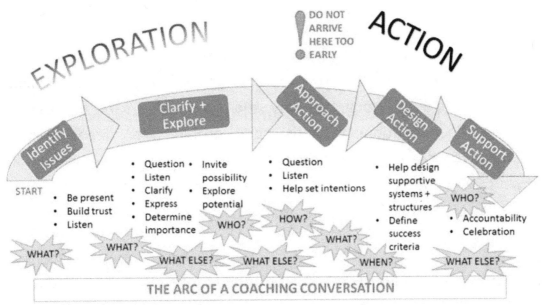

Figure 3- the arc of a coaching conversation[6]

Project Stakeholders

Scott W Ambler defines Stakeholders[7] as " anyone who is a direct, indirect user, manager of users, senior manager, operation staff member, the "gold owner" who funds the project, support (help desk) staff members, auditors, your program portfolio manager, developers working on other systems that integrate or interact with the one under development, or maintenance professionals potentially affected by the development and/or deployment of a software" So people directly impacted or potentially affected by the changes done to the software under development. I really like the stakeholder categorization done by **Carl Kessler** and **John Sweitzer** on their book **Outside-in Software Development**[8], also mentioned by **Scott W Ambler** on the article referred above:

- Principals (the people who buy your software),
- End-users (the people who interact with it),
- Partners (the people who will make your software work in production),
- Insiders (people within your organization that impact how your team works).

---

[6] Sue Johnston, "The Arc of a Coaching Conversation"
[7] Scott W Ambler, "Active Stakeholder Participation: An Agile Best Practice",
http://agilemodeling.com/essays/activeStakeholderParticipation.htm
[8] Carl Kessler, John Sweitzer, Outside-in Software Development: A Practical Approach to Building Successful Stakeholder-based Products Paperback – Sep 24 2007

Stakeholders are responsible for the project, product or service that the team will be working with. Its participation and permanent support to the product that would be develop and the team that would be behind of it would be crucial along this stage of the team's transformation process. This role is crucial given that they would challenge what product owners would do along the way and collaborate with the team to build appropriated product solutions to solve their problems or needs. Regarding the stakeholders and their expectations about the team that would be formed, I like to ask only the main stakeholder, to join the Product Owner and meet to discuss about **Product development expectations**, in a meeting that it's explained below.

Product Owner

The Product owner, it's responsible and accountable for the project, product or service that the team will be working with. This role matters because money wise these people are making decisions about what would be delivered, why now and when it should happen. Their capacity to oversee how their product or service would look like in the future, how to plan efficiently to get there and how that is communicated, pass through what kind of team they think its needed to reach established business goals. I'm referring here to expected team attitude and behaviour, how problems get resolved, the team's capacity to deliver on time, the team's capacity to perform under pressure and their ability to adapt to continuous changes. Here some techniques that I like using to help with setting clear expectations about the product, the team and how we are going to work together:

Product development meeting

What's the purpose of it?

- Get to know each other better
- Discuss about the product/service vision
- Clarify expectations about the team, in terms of:
    - Attitudes and behaviours
    - Communication style (Command and control/Open communication)
    - Collaboration (Restricted/Completely open)

Clarify expectation about how we are going to work together:

- Role and responsibilities
- How to collaborate towards reaching amazing results.

- Everything else that you considered makes sense for your specific context

Expected outcome
- Product Owner and Scrum Master/Agile Coach way to work has been established.
- Stakeholder team expectation has been discussed and clarified.
- Product Owner and Stakeholder way to work has been established.

> **Tip:** If there is no Product Vision available, I strongly recommend start discussing about the goals of the product for the next three (3) months and make that visible for the team. You could use *the **Team's Road Map template*** presented below, *to help you out with it.*

Product planning weekly based meeting

What's the purpose of it?
- Assist/Support with keeping the team focused on what's important.
- Assist/Support with keeping the Product Backlog iteration planning ready.
- Help with visualizing what's next in the product pipeline.
- Create inspect and adapt mindset about the product.
- Assist/Support with creating the Product Vision.
- Create product planning habits.

> **Tip:** This is good opportunity to explain and discuss about what your role and responsibilities are, regarding the team. Avoid assuming that the Product Owner understands what the scope of your role is. Share details about commanding-controlling versus influencing and empowering instead. When do you intervene and why it's important to let the team learn from failure

Expected outcome
- The Product has been planned and the Product Owner is able to communicate what's next to stakeholders and then to the team.

From what I've seen in the field, Product Owners wants to rely on a team who delivers results consistently, as soon as possible, so please let's remember that when working together with them as our main goal.

> 💡 **Tip:** If there is a Product Road-map available, I strongly recommend start discussing about it, in order to help the Product owner set what's next for the team. If there is no Product Road-map available, you could use *the team's Product Road Map template* presented below, to help you out with it. In any case, it's highly recommended to bring this artifact to the meeting and ask to be updated.

Line Managers

Line manager(s) main role is to support their employees' activities by providing them the required tools needed to do their job. In an agile environment, there is an additional support required and that is for the development process. Line manager's capacity to allow Scrum Masters/Agile coaches do their job, and the ability to empower teams to self-organize their work, would be a key factor to consider when working with teams. Here some techniques that I like using to help with setting clear expectations about management roles, how to support the team and how to collaborate with the Scrum Master/Agile Coach:

Touch base regularly

I used to have monthly one on one with Line managers where we discus about how the team is doing, what the biggest road blockers are and what's my Scrum Master/Agile Coach perception about their happiness.

- **Benefits:** Meeting often helps with increasing collaboration between the Scrum Master and the line manager, brings insights about their employees, create opportunities for crucial conversations and speed up the decision-making process not matter how things are doing for the employees.
- **Potential risks:** Monthly meetings are time consuming and it could be challenging to keep the mechanism ongoing, when working with more than two teams at the same time.

Keep the collaboration channel open

Especially in agile setups, Line manager's need to be creative to find ways to connect and discuss with their teams, without interrupting their flow or becoming impediments to their job. Something that I have tried is to allow especial time at the end of the iterations, I mean after the iteration review and before the iteration retrospective, where they would discuss openly with the team about how things are doing.

- **Benefits:** What I've experienced is that line managers love to get in touch with their employees and having the time to do it, allows them to connect and build the relationship of trust. For the employee, it could become a timeframe to express issues, ideas or feelings about the job directly with his/her manager. This mechanism could save money and reduce overturns when referring to people leaving the company.
- **Potential risks:** It could be perceived as a waste of time, especially for the Product Owners.

From what I have seen in the field, Line Managers wants you to help them with *forming agile teams* that delivers high quality results consistently and do it faster, so please let's remember that when working with them along this stage of the team's transformation process.

The Kick-Off meeting

Now, it is time for you to create the team's transformation process project charter and get ready for the kick-off meeting. Here the elements to be considered when building project charter:

Team's Transformation Process Project Charter Template

What's this project about?

I.e. The cars division wants to rely on team that's able to deliver any kind of work any time on time and within the forecasted budget.

Why are we doing it right now?

Reason	Strategy
E.g. Focus on what brings value to the division in order to increase the Return of Investment per project	E.g. Optimize where the company put its efforts by distributing properly the content to be integrated.
E.g. Increase operational efficiency	E.g. Improve project planning and prioritization at the Product team level
	E.g. Increase collaboration with directors and different stakeholders
	E.g. Build a high performing sustainable development team

Figure 4-Team's Transforming Process Project Charter-Reasons

Vision of the team 1 year from now

- E.g. a fully collaborative and cross functional team is in place.
- E.g. every member of the development team can work on any project at any time.
- E.g. knowledge is shared within the team and that's done via development process.
- E.g. a high-performing sustainable development team is in place.

Main goals for the next three (3) months

- E.g. Team`s Development process is implemented end to end
- E.g. Development team backlog is healthy (Properly prioritized based what the business wants and what brings more value)

Roles and responsibilities

Role	Responsibilities
Main Stakeholder (Full name)	E.g. sets high level vision for the content to be developed. E.g. negotiates priorities with Customers. E.g. helps Product Owners make the vision and corporate goals tangible in the development team backlog
Product/Service Owner (Full name)	E.g. manages development team Backlog E.g. decides what to do and when (Establishes backlog priorities) E.g. negotiates priorities with main Stakeholder E.g. leads development team to deliver the content of its backlog E.g. collaborates with the Agile Coach/Scrum Master in order to create a high-performing sustainable team. E.g. collaborates with the delivery team with refining the development team's backlog
Agile Coach/Scrum Master (Full name)	E.g. Sheppard's team's development process E.g. coaches the team to become a self-organizing and high-performing sustainable team E.g. coaches Product Owners with managing the team's backlog and with leading the team. E.g. facilitates all team ceremonies E.g. facilitates interactions between team members E.g. removes impediments from the way of the team
Development team (Name of the team or description)	E.g. does the job to (description of what the team does) .... E.g. delivers high-quality _____for <division/unit/client> E.g. collaborates with Product Owners and the Agile Coach/Scrum Master to increase team's performance E.g. raises impediments and make them visible to the team.
Line team manager(s) Full Name	E.g. brings support to the team and the development process E.g. collaborates with the Agile Coach/Scrum Master with removing impediments
Stakeholders (List of all stakeholders)	E.g. collaborates with the team and the Product team with grooming the content of the development team backlog

Figure 5-Team's Transforming Process Project Charter -Roles and responsibilities

High level Risks

Risk Category	Description
Human Resources	E.g. people's resistance to change
Communication	E.g. limited support from Stakeholders and PO's.
Communication	E.g. unclear goals, and unshared vision
Communication	E.g. unclear roles and responsibilities
Resources	E.g. project loses interest and stakeholder stop funding it

Figure 6-Team's Transforming Process Project Charter -High level risks

<u>Process high level guidelines</u>

I.e. This team has been using Kanban as their way to deal with requirements. There are no special events, no time boxed iterations are set and no feedback loop in place.

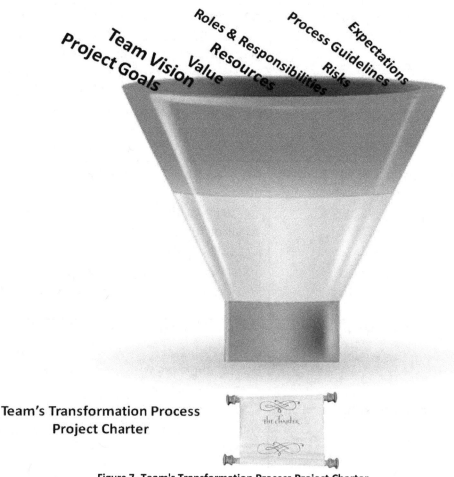

Team's Transformation Process
Project Charter

Figure 7- Team's Transformation Process Project Charter

Kick-off meeting setup

Once the Team's transformation Process Project Charter got completed is time to set up for the kick-off meeting. Here some of the elements to take in consideration:

1. Share and discuss the document with the main stakeholder, the line managers and the Product Owner(s).
2. Verify that everybody is OK with its content.
3. Organize the kick-off meeting agenda.
4. Schedule the meeting
5. Be sure that all parties involved get invited.

During the Kick-off meeting

At this stage of the process, the Team's Transformation Process Project Charter has been created, the Kick-off meeting has been setup and the day has come to start interacting frequently with your new team. In order to facilitate this process, I like to follow this agenda during the kick-off meeting:

Agenda	Responsible
1. Kick-off meeting's goal	Product Owner/Main Stakeholder

2. Team's Transformation Process Project
 	
   a. What this project is about
 	
   b. Why we are doing it right now
 	
   c. Vision of the team 1 year from now
 	
   d. Main goals for the next three (3) months
	Product Owner/Main Stakeholder

3. Team's Transformation Process Project **Roles & Responsibilities**	Scrum Master/Agile Coach
4. Team's Transformation Process Project **High Level Risks**	Scrum Master/Agile Coach

Figure 8 - Team's Transformation Process Project - Kick off Agenda

The Development team

Once the project has kicked-off and the leadership team has been approached, the main focus is the development team and how to start working together. With a little help of the Product/Service owner and the development group/team, I would find ways to get to know them as much as possible. Here some techniques that I use when approaching the team and start building the relationship of trust:

Get introduced by somebody already trusted

After asking the leadership team, and a couple of quick chats, it would be nice to ask that person that is already trusted by the team, to introduce you to the group. Using this reference, would influence people's opinions, ease assumptions and avoid unnecessary judgements to could get in the way of creating an amazing and productive relationship based on trust. If that's not possible, I love to ask another Scrum Master (if available) to do it for me.

- **Benefits:** I haven't invented this, and this is what I use when meeting others to get closer to them. I see it like this: If I trust you and you trust him/her then I will trust him/her.
- **Potential risks:** It requires the right attitude, the right people and it's highly contextual based, so there is an elevated risk that this technique doesn't work.

> 💡 **Tip:** This act is really important, so please paying attention to details matters here. I would strongly recommend going with your common sense. Imagine this act as the most important event of your future work relationship, so be your more authentic self and listen to them first.

Be humble and listen

At the moment that you join a new team, people start to observe how you behave. It's normal to expect that people would try you in different ways and with different things during this stage of the group development. Group acceptance, knowledge validation, shared interests and leadership still would be under testing in this face, so please be humble and listen actively to what their trying to say.

- **Benefits:** As much as they feel listened and that you're not a thread to them and that you're there to help them with honesty, you would gain their trust and they will slowly open up to you.

> 💡 **Tip:** *"Your job here is to create the container and let them create the content and remember that it's not about you, it's about them"*

- **Potential risks:** Personal attacks from people dysfunctional behaviors could be recurrent here and could make you and the feel uncomfortable, just remember.

> 💡 **Tip:** *"It's not about you; it's what you represent to them, so please do yourself a favor and don't take it personal"*
> Omar Bermudez, Coaching session, Montreal **2013**

Give you time to observe

If you're the type let's go and change the world today and tomorrow everything would work fine, well I think that you will learn soon about this way to go. Instead what I do is to take at least a full iteration to just observe and take notes about how the team works, interact and how is everything happening for the team.

- **Benefits:** Giving yourself time to observe the team, would offer you the chance to have a better comprehension about the system that the team has become. It would give you insights to validate how to proceed in the future. It would also get you a closer look about who's playing which role in the team, and that could lead to ideas about how to approach individuals next.

- **Potential risks:** This could create the perception that you're doing nothing to help the team, so be careful and communicate your strategies before to everybody involved in the transformation project.

Be actively present, on time and ready to rock

If you want to build a relationship of trust with the team, behave showing the example that you want the team to follow. That means, be present physically and mentally 100% of the time. Put your cellphone, tablet and any potential distraction away, and be there for them. Be on time and respect your commitments no matter what they do. You want them to see that something new is about to start happening, and that starts with you first showing what to do. Get ready to rock, which means be prepared to jump in and start helping them. It could be facilitating a conversation or just writing things in a board, just be ready to do what you love the most.

- **Benefits**: By being present you show that you care about them, and people would appreciate that and that would help with building the relationship of trust. Being on time shows respect for the process, for the environment and for another people time. That would also help with building the relationship of trust with the team and would help them to follow and do the same. Being always ready to rock would demonstrate your disposition to help them when it's needed and that would create support and a baseline for a strong relationship of trust too.

- **Potential risks:** Becoming impatient and try to fix people behaviour could diminish all your efforts and destroy what has been built in seconds. Be careful.

3. Iteration Planning

What is the Iteration Planning for?

It's the event for planning what the team has forecasted to complete for the customer by the end of the iteration. It's also the time for the team to set the iteration goal, and to discus and agree upon the iteration backlog.

When is the Iteration Planning held?

It's held at the beginning of the iteration.

Who Participates in the Iteration Planning and How?

Here is what I've found that works better for each role when participating in the iteration planning:

Role	Responsibilities

Product Owner	- Prepares the content of the top product backlog items with the help of the Scrum Master.
	- Explains what the iteration goal is to the team (It's nice to share the reasons behind the choice with the team).
	- Exposes and discusses its Product/Service wish list for the iteration.
	- Encourages collaboration between the stakeholders and the development team about the future of the product.
	- Listens carefully to what the team wants to say in terms of:
	    • User stories dependencies;
	    • Potential risks;
	    • Potential roadblocks;
	    • Task complexity.
	- Is open to receive and give answers to the team about the content of the Product Backlog and its priorities.
	- Negotiates the final iteration commitment with the team.
	- Collaborates with the Scrum Master with creating a safe environment to increase collaboration, visibility and transparency.

Figure 9- Iteration Planning - Product Owner Role & Responsibilities

Role	Responsibilities
Scrum Master/Agile Coach	- Ensures that the event happens at the same time at the end of the iteration. - Facilitates collaboration between the Development Team, the Product Owner and Other Specialists in the room. - Creates a safe environment to contain the event and empowers collaboration. - Ensures that the meeting is structured and stays focused. - Identifies potential issues that are required to be addressed later and asks for responsible people before the meeting ends. - Ensures that meeting stays within the established time frame. - Coach/Mentor/Teach the Product Owner with writing the Iteration Goal. - Coach/Mentor/Teach the Development Team with splitting tasks in small chunks of work. - Coach/Mentor/Teach the Scrum Team on how to calculate the team's capacity. - Coach/Mentor/Teach the Development Team with deciding what to commit to and how to accomplish it.

Figure 10-Iteration Planning - Scrum Master/Agile Coach Role & Responsibilities

Role	Responsibilities
Development Team	- Challenges the Product Owner's wish list. - Raise concerns regarding potential issues that could get in the way of the team reaching the iteration goal. - Proposes solutions and provides expert technological advice to the Product Owner. - Collaborates to get the iteration planning completed. - Collaborates with updating the Definition of Done. - Grooms product backlog items as required. - Listens carefully what the Product Owner is saying about the Product Backlog. - Answers questions related to the iteration content. - Breaks down every single product backlog item into small tasks and assigns an estimate in hours to it. - Decides high level strategies to tackle the iteration.

Figure 11-Iteration Planning -Development Team Role & Responsibilities

What kind of techniques could be used to improving the Iteration Planning?

Structure your Iteration planning
Help the team by offering some kind of structure to work with during the Iteration Planning.

Keep the Product Backlog refined and groom often
This could help your team(s) to reduce waste during the iteration and stay focused on what needs to be done.

In order to accomplish this, you would:

1. Have **at least one two-hour Product Backlog refinement session** per two weeks of iteration.

2. For the Scrum Master to help and support the Product Owner weekly regarding the content of the Product Backlog based on the Product Roadmap (At the very least, a high-level vision of the upcoming three months of work).

3. **Use the Team's Roadmap template** to help you when assisting the Product Owner with setting Product Backlog priorities and make them visible for the team.

4. **Avoid being so rigid and purist about scrum practices**. Where people are involved, instead use and trust your common sense and even trust some of their ideas.

5. **Skip the ceremony on purpose**. Something that I sometimes do, is miss the beginning of the iteration planning, so the team can figure it out by themselves. The first time you do this, it would be awkward, but after some time the team will get used to it.

6. **Repeat, repeat and repeat**. Keep using these techniques until the team starts owning them.

7. **Have fun.** Enjoy what you do, talk with your team(s) about people's lives, what is happening around the world, and take the time to connect with them

Iteration Planning Template - Overview

Summary - Part A

Suggested Steps	
Purpose	**Techniques**
STEP 1 - Build Community	
Helps the team with creating the bond required to move on together	• Get the room prepared (Meeting agenda is visible to everybody in the room, everything is set) • Welcome the scrum team to the room, make them feel safe by saying good morning/afternoon • Ask an open-ended powerful question to warm them up: i.e.: What's new in our lives? What about your weekend?
STEP 2 - Close Previous Iteration	
Helps the team with creating awareness about what happened previous iteration	• Ask permission to the team to go over previous iteration results, which means • Revise iteration burn down to validate how the iteration went and ask/tell the team to look for patterns that could lead the team to improve
W H Y / **W H A T**	• Ask the Product Owner to set its expectations for the iteration by establishing the main focus of it. • Ask the Product Owner to share the iteration goal with the development team • Help the development team challenge the Product Owner iteration goal by asking open ended questions
	• Be sure that everything in the backlog is ready to be planned. If there is something to be discussed, go for it. Ask the team if they feel OK to include the item into the iteration backlog and look for signs of confirmation: Check the team's behaviour and watch them to validate if that match their speech.
	• Ask the Product Owner to go over of the iteration wish list. • Open the floor for questions about why we are doing this wish list. Challenge priorities until the team gets common understanding • Remember: this is an iterative process, so you would get the team to do it step by step

Figure 12- Iteration Planning Template suggested steps - Part A

Iteration Planning Template - Overview

Summary - Part B

Suggested Steps	
Purpose	**Techniques**
Step 3 - Do we need a break before moving on?	
Helps with creating the step back to think mindset in the team	• Ask the team to include breaks in the agenda iteration planning agenda and then stick to it. • Make sure that it happens when planned.
Step 4 - Calculate Team's capacity [Iteration level]	
Establishes limits to help the team with focusing on what's possible to be delivered	• I do use team's median velocity and man hours to help team assess how accurate it's the amount of work that the team is committing to deliver. Here is a formula that could help you with calculating • Teams Capacity in hours for the iteration: • (#Workable Hours x day) *(#Workable Days of the iteration) *(#Workable Days x developer) *(#Developers working)
Step 5- Task breakdown	
It's the development team's time to discuss about how to do the job in order to reach the iteration goal	• Let the team break down every single item identified in the Product Owner Wish list in tasks (<=1 day. Duration). Ask the team to estimate how long it will take to complete each task in hours, in order to compare with the calculated Team Capacity in man hours. Once the team is done, challenge the iteration commitment comparing the number of hours that team committed to do with the calculated team capacity. Do the same with the amount of Story Points that the team is committing to deliver and the median Velocity of the team.
Step 6 - Close the Iteration planning	
Helps the team give some visibility and be challenged about what's going to be delivered (the plan)	• Ask the development team to present to the Product Owner what would be the iteration commitment (what they are expecting to deliver by the end of the iteration). Ask if it make sense for everybody in the room and verify with the Product Owner if the iteration backlog priorities are OK. Now the team is ready to start the iteration!

Figure 13- Iteration Planning Template suggested steps - Part B

Instructions

Before the meeting

1. Chose an empty board in the room where the iteration planning would be held
2. Create a personal **Kanban**[9] with three columns (To do, Discussing and Done) on it
3. In a Super sticky note (I like 4 in x 4 in), right down the **iteration planning template** suggested steps, one step sticky note.
4. Place all your super sticky note **iteration planning template** suggested steps, below the To-Do column of your personal Kanban board.

During the meeting

1. Once the meeting has started, move into the "Discussing" column of your personal Kanban board, the **iteration planning template** suggested step that is being discussed at the moment.
2. When the "Discussion" is done, move the **iteration planning template** suggested step to the "Done" column.
3. Repeat steps 1 and 2 until each **iteration planning template** step has been discussed.

---

[9] Kanban, https://en.wikipedia.org/wiki/Kanban

Visual Instructions

Before the Meeting			During the Meeting		
To do	**Doing**	**Done**	**To do**	**Doing**	**Done**

Build Community

Close Previous Sprint

Sprint Goal

Grooming

Product Wish List

break

Calculate Team's Capacity

Task breakdown

Close Sprint Planning

Build Community

Close Previous Sprint

Sprint Goal

Product Wish List

break

Calculate Team's Capacity

Task breakdown

Close Sprint Planning

Figure 14-Visual Instructions Iteration Planning Template

Simple Explanation

✔	Main Steps	WHY
	Build Community	Helps establish the bond required to move forward as a unit.
	Close Previous Iteration	Create awareness about what happened during the previous iteration.
	Define/Set Iteration Goal	Iteration WHAT and WHY
	Product Backlog Grooming/Refining	
	Product Owner Wish List	
	Break Required	Helps with creating the step back to think mindset in the team
	Calculate Team's Capacity [Iteration level]	Establishes limits to help the team with focusing on what's possible to be delivered
	Task Breakdown	Development team time to discuss about how to do the job in order to reach the iteration goal
	Close the Iteration planning	Helps the team give some visibility and be challenged about what's going to be Delivered (the plan)

Figure 15- Iteration Planning Template - Simple Explanation

Detailed Explanation

✔	Main Steps	Techniques
	Build Community	• Prepare room by ensuring all artifacts are clear and visible prior to the meeting • Welcome and thank the team Warm up the room by asking powerful open-ended questions.
	Close Previous Iteration	• Close previous Iteration Review the team's previous iteration results with their permission
	Define/Set Iteration Goal	• Product Owner has established the iterations main focus and expectations • Product Owner to communicate/share the iterations main focus and expectations Development team to challenge/question (WHY?) the iterations main focus and expectations
	Product Backlog Grooming/Refining	• Review with team/PO that the backlog is ready to be planned. Must discuss and remove ambiguities. Validate with the team if they feel OK to include the item into the iteration backlog • Look for signs of confirmation (Body Language matches oral communication): Check the team's behaviour and watch them to validate if that match their speech.
	Product Owner Wish List	• The Product Owner to communicate the iterations wish list. The team to question about why we are doing that wish list. Challenge priorities until the team gets common understanding (Remember: this is an iterative process, so you would get the team to do it step by step) Pay attention to those teams that don't challenge as it might be, it could be a sign to take care after.
	Break Required	• Ask the team to include breaks in the agenda iteration planning agenda and then stick to it. Make sure that it happens when planned.

Figure 16 - Iteration Planning Template - Detailed Explanation Part 1

Detailed Explanation (cont.)

✔	Main Steps	Techniques
	Calculate Team's Capacity [Iteration level]	• Use the team's median velocity and man hours to help team assess how accurate it's the amount of work that the team is committing to deliver. Here is a formula that could help you with calculating Teams Capacity in hours for the iteration: (#Workable Hours x day) *(#Workable Days of the iteration) *(#Workable Days x developer) *(#Developers working)
	Task Breakdown	• Let the team break down every single item identified in the Product Owner Wish list in tasks • (<=1 day. Duration). Ask the team to estimate how long it will take to complete each task in hours, in order to compare with the calculated Team Capacity in man hours. Once the team is done, challenge the iteration commitment comparing the number of hours that team committed to do with the calculated team capacity. Do the same with the amount of Story Points that the team will commit to deliver and the median Velocity of the team.
	Close the Iteration planning	• Ask the development team to present to the Product Owner what would be the iteration commitment (what they are expecting to deliver by the end of the iteration). • Ask if it make sense for everybody in the room and verify with the Product Owner if the iteration backlog priorities are OK. Now the team is ready to start the iteration!

Figure 17- Iteration Planning Template - Detailed Explanation Part 2

4. Iteration Daily Sync

What is the daily sync about?

The Daily sync is considered as the "event for the development team to synchronize activities and create a plan for the next 24 hours" within the Scrum guide[10].

For **Martin Fowler**[11] the "daily stand-up meetings have become a ritual of many agile teams, especially in Agile Software development". Martin refers to it[12], as the time where "the whole agile team meets every day for a quick status update. We stand up to keep the meeting short".

In my opinion, this is a decision-making moment where the team inspects the status of the work in progress, raises impediments that are on the way of reaching the goal of the iteration, and collaborates to get the work done. It's suggested to keep it short, in order to avoid dispersion, to reduce ambiguity and increase the team's efficiency by clarifying who does what.

When is the daily sync held?

It really depends on the team. In my experience, most agile teams hold it daily at the beginning of the workday and it's up to them to decide where and at what time.

In my experience, I like to suggest that my teams keep the daily sync fixed; this means the same time and the same place, in order to facilitate that it became a habit for the team.

What's the goal of the daily sync?

There are several goals for a daily sync meeting. In my opinion, if the agile team is able to answer the question "Where are we in the iteration?" with a couple of phrases; that's a sign that everybody is on the same page, which for me is the main goal of the meeting. This meeting provides visibility on potential delays and obstacles for the agile team. **Martin Fowler** has identified five (5) goals for a daily sync meeting as **GIFTS**, a mnemonic device to facilitate the daily sync meeting and achieve goals learning:

---

[10] The Scrum Guide, http://www.scrumguides.org/scrum-guide.html
[11] Martin Fowler, http://martinfowler.com/aboutMe.html
[12] Martin Fowler, "Is not just standing up", http://martinfowler.com/articles/itsNotJustStandingUp.html

Good start (help start the day well)

Improvement (support improvement)

Focus (reinforce focus on the right things)

Team (reinforce the sense of team)

Status (communicate what is going on)

Figure 18 - GIFTS

Who participates in the daily sync and how?

Here is what I've found works better for each role when participating during the iteration daily sync:

Role	Responsibilities
Product Owner	- Its presence is optional but extremely recommended. - Supports the development team self-organization by letting them manages how things are done. - Protects team against priorities changes and context switching during the iteration. - Collaborates with the development team to get things done. - Answers development team questions. - Validates work progression/done with the development team. - Reassess iteration priorities with the development team. - Helps the team stay on track during the iteration. - Challenges development team when since are not progressing as expected. - Collaborates with the Scrum Master/Agile Coach to make the meeting happen daily.

Figure 19-Iteration Daily Sync - Product Owner role and responsibilities

Role	Responsibilities
Stakeholder(s)	- Its presence is optional. - Asks/Answers team questions once the meeting is done by the development team - Collaborates with the Scrum Master/Agile coach with creating a safe environment to increase collaboration, visibility and transparency. - Supports team self-organization and let them manages how things are done. - Helps the team remove impediments and stay on track during the iteration. - Challenges development team when since are not progressing as expected. - Collaborates with the Scrum Master/Agile Coach to make the meeting happen daily.

Figure 20- Iteration Daily Sync Stakeholder(s) role and responsibilities

Role	Responsibilities
Scrum Master/Agile coach	- Ensures that the act happens at the same time and at the same place after agreement with the team. - Facilitates collaboration between the development team, the Product owner and the stakeholders. - Creates a safe environment to contain the event and empowers collaboration. - Ensures that the meeting is structured and stays focused. - Identify potential issues that require to be addressed later and ask for responsible before the meeting ends. - Ensures that meeting stays within established time box. - Helps the agile team to deliver results by challenging the work progress. - Helps the agile team with removing impediments out of their way. - Teach/Coach the Team alternatives for keeping the meeting energized. - Teach/Coach the team techniques to improve the quality of the daily sync.

Figure 21-Iteration Daily Sync - Scrum Master/Agile Coach role and responsibilities

Role	Responsibilities
Specialist(s)	- Contributes with the team to get things done by answering any questions that could become impediments to reach iterations goal. - Similar responsibilities like the Development team but I haven't seen often these people challenging the "What" and the "Why". What I've seen instead, is them answering specific technical questions to clarify system related requirements.

Figure 22-Iteration Daily Sync - Specialist(s) role and responsibilities

What techniques could be used to getting the best out of the daily sync?

A daily sync meeting is a short meeting, which occurs daily (it's recommended that it is completed in less than 15 minutes) where the development team meets to:

Start the day

Starting the day fresh is an amazing way to get organized for the challenges that will come, so let's stand up and have a talk with our agile teammates. It helps the agile team to get used to planning ahead and sets sharing and collaboration as the way to go when working with the team.

How to do it?

I like to show up at the precise time that the agile team agreed the daily sync would happen. I don't say a word; I just stand there in the middle of the war room. Then I wait until someone stands up, and then the rest will follow. I repeat this for a couple of weeks until the agile team gets the habit and does it on their own.

Suggested attitude

I strongly recommend that you be ready to act. Have breakfast early so that your body is sparking with enough energy to light up the entire room. Be there and challenge them to engage in one of the most important conversations of the day. Please smile, remember smiles are free!

<u>Reinforce the focus on the right things</u>

People enjoy engaging in deep technical discussions, especially during the daily sync. That's cool, but the agile team has the whole day to do that, so let's keep it light and energized. If you see someone engaging in a deep technical discussion, let it finish, and by the end of the daily sync meeting ask permission to share some observations; by high-lighting how that deep technical discussion contributed to the purpose of the daily sync or whether it did not contribute.

How to do it?

First of all, let them talk and remember it is their meeting not yours. Allow the agile team to talk freely but once the meeting is done, ask them "How do you think it went?"

Then stick to the following rules:

SRFLV (Short and simple, Raise impediments, Fun, Light, Visible)

I find these rules helpful to create awareness about the purpose of the meeting and its importance for the agile team.

Use provided tools. Refer to the **GIFTS** goals and ask them for help to keep learning and improving.

Short and simple (keep it short and simple)

Raise impediments (make impediments visible)

Fun (have fun when do it)

Light (keep it light)

Visible (make things visible)

Figure 23- Reinforce the focus on the right things

Make progress toward the iteration goal visible to the team

Some of the best agile teams that I've worked with have two boards to keep track of how the iteration is progressing. A physical board and an electronic version which represents what the agile team has agreed to get done during the iteration content. I love a physical board, because people can interact with it and in my experience, it facilitates interactions and makes the agile team grow by collaborating. It brings a sense of ownership too. By owning a physical board, where their own ideas would be shown, provides a sense of control of the destiny of the people in the team. So, encourage them to make things visible as a simple way to control what they do. Invite them to make things visible and keep progress updated, so that decisions can be made sooner than later during the iteration.

How to do it?

If the agile team has decided to use a physical board to track their work, then once the board is up, I will show them what the agile team is expected to do, in order to keep the meeting efficient. First, physically refer to the card (Product Backlog Item) that the person is planning to work on and share information to answer the three questions that follow:

1. What have you done since yesterday regarding the iteration?
2. What's the plan for today?
3. What are the road blockers on your way to get the iteration done?

What if we decide to engage into a technical conversation?

Depending on how many people are in the agile team, I'll let the conversation go on, until it reaches the 15 minutes timeline. Then, I'll ask the agile team to share what they have noticed about the conversation going on as long as it did and are you still able to tell me, where we are in the iteration? If the answer is unclear or ambiguous, I take that as a sign that the meeting needs some work.

What about agile team members arriving late, showing up with a non-collaborative attitude?

I would love to tell you that I have an answer for that, but I don't! My suggestion in this case would be to try and look for a cause of what is behind the person's dysfunctional behavior. Be curious and try to get that person's attention to have a conversation about what you've observed during the daily sync. I strongly recommend that you follow this path if you have validated that the dysfunctional behavior is a pattern and other people in the agile team; other than you, have noticed too.

> 💡 **Tip:** An issue becomes an issue if someone else can see it; other than you. So rely on facts to support your interventions in order to increase your success rate when facing people's dysfunctional behavior.

Raise impediments that could impact the agile team to reach the iteration goal.

To be honest, creating the habit of raising impediments with agile teams is hard. People react to it! I think it's because weaknesses can be perceived by others, like if you aren't capable of getting things done. Believe me, I've used different approaches, different ways and there is not a common practice that I can share with you. However, I like to explain to them that raising impediments is our only way to get things done by collaborating with the rest of the organization.

How to do it?

During the first meetings, I ask them at the end of the meeting: What are the team's road blocks today regarding the iteration?

Suggested attitude

By the end of the daily sync meeting, I like to express my curiosity by asking some powerful questions[13] to the agile team regarding the iteration, for example: Where are we in the iteration? (Ahead, on or off schedule) What about the iteration goal? Where are we with it, off or on track? Is there anything blocking the agile team's path to reach the iteration goal? I strongly recommend that you closely observe people's attitudes when you ask these powerful questions. Look for patterns, non-verbal communication, and receptiveness. Remain open to suggestions and make your intentions clear by sharing why are you asking all of these questions. I would also say for you to be patient and keep your verbiage short too.

Communicate Daily syncs are all about communicating what's going on within the agile team, specifically regarding the iteration and its progression. I like to encourage the agile team to talk, be open, and provide the space for them to do it.

---

[13] Powerful questions, Lyssa Adkins, "Powerful questions for agile teams", http://www.coachingagileteams.com/2008/04/15/agile/powerful-questions-for-agile-teams/

How to do it?

Focus on the container, not on the content. Invite them to fill the 'container' with their comments by sharing their ideas. I always look for inspiration and what motivates them to share. Some people are visual, others prefer to sense it and others like to hear about it. Observe and be curious about their interests and focus on creating the safest environment possible and you'll see them flourish.

Cheer the team on

Motivated people are open to learning; that leads to creativity and innovation. So be up for it and cheer them on but pay attention and please be real. Feel it, so then you can inspire them to feel it too.

Support improvement

Invite the agile team to guide their destiny and to own their space, by answering the question: what else can we do to help him excel in the daily sync meeting? Be there for them to support their work and make him/her be a leader for the team. I love to see it this way:

More help accepted => more trust established => higher collaboration=> Incredible results

Let it go and observe how it goes

After the 5th week since the agile team has started having daily sync meetings, and only for testing purposes, I like to be absent from the meetings, so the team can figure it out by themselves. Then, I ask the Product Owner, do you know where we are in the iteration? Do you need anything from me or from the team? And then I'll rely on those answers to build from there and continue helping the agile team to improve.

Apply "Tom fades out" technique

I've developed a technique called "Tom fades out" which refers to the fact that I'll be close by the agile team during the first few daily syncs. But then, I'll tend to get out of their field of visibility to allow them to see each other and facilitate direct interactions. After a couple of months of doing it, you'll see that you won't need to be there physically standing with them, they will do it by themselves.

And last but not least, please **repeat, repeat and repeat.** I've learned by practicing over and over again, people get used to doing things and end up by incorporating those practices as part of their own lives.

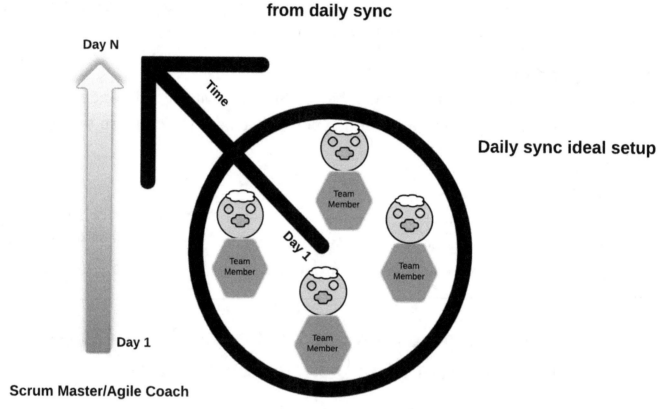

Figure 24-Tom fades out from daily sync

5. Helping the team to stay focused

What is the team's focus?

Once the iteration has started, the main goal of the agile team is to reach the iteration goal; discussed and established in the iteration planning process. But how do we do it? The key is to maintain focus on the iteration during the whole process.

How to do to keep the team focused?

Set the iteration goal together

During the iteration planning, I like to invite the Product Owner to write the iteration goal on a big colourful post-it. Once written, it's the turn of the Development Team to validate it, given that it would be the team's main focus during the iteration. In addition, I use a couple of open-ended questions; to guarantee that the Product Owner doesn't take advantage of the team in cases where there are multiple goals to be attained:

- What would be the main goal of the iteration?
- From all these goals, what is the one that the team can't drop?

Make the iteration goal visible

At the moment that the iteration goal has been established, I invite the Product Owner to bring the iteration goal post-it to the team's 'war room' and put it in a place where it will be visible and the team will see it every day. Depending on the company, visible wall areas are sometimes not accessible to be changed. If that's the case, invite the main stakeholder to share with the team, which area could be owned by the team in order to make the work visible. If that's impossible, you can use rolling whiteboards[14] instead. I love these, they are amazing because people can draw on it, it can be moved anywhere in the office, and what I find awesome is the fact that the team can own it and by doing that, it becomes a piece of real estate of the team's world.

Physical task boards

The best teams that I've worked with have used physical task boards during the forming stage. **Tom Perry**[15] defines a physical task board as "the single most important

---

[14] Rolling Whiteboards, http://www.amazon.com/Offex-Dry-Erase-Magnetic-Whiteboard-Casters/dp/B007NFDEQC
[15] Tom Perry, https://agiletools.wordpress.com/about/

information radiator that an agile team has. A task board illustrates the progress that an agile team is making in achieving their sprint/iteration goals."[16]

There are multiple benefits expected when a team use a physical task board:

- It ensures efficient diffusion of relevant information to the whole team.
- It facilitates discussions during the daily sync meeting, serving as the central point.
- It keeps daily sync meetings focused on progress and obstacles.
- Its simplicity and flexibility enable a team's collaboration and makes the decision-making process faster and incredibly efficient.
- It allows the team to present relevant information easily by using post-its, markers, and other affordable elementary materials.

"The task board is an expression of the personality of the team"

Tom Perry, Task Boards: Telling a compelling

But be careful and challenge the agile team

Some teams fall into the trap of avoiding making their work visible for the rest of the team. When that happens, teams tend to blame that the board is not helping them, for example or that it makes their lives too complicated. So please remember, that each one of us is a special and unique human being, so reactions to new things and changes will be different and that's ok.

How to deal with that?

Don't do it for them; instead invite them to see how others do it within the company; if you're lucky enough to work in a place where other teams are using physical task boards already. If not, then have the team take a look the **list of physical task boards**[17] that was gathered by **Tom Perry**, to inspire them. Present them with the benefits first and show them how easy and fun work can be just by adding this tool to what the team does. In conclusion, let the team build their physical task board.

Coach the team to raise impediments

---

[16] Tom Perry, "Task Boards: telling a compelling agile story",https://agiletools.wordpress.com/2007/11/24/task-boards-telling-a-compelling-agile-story/

[17] Tom Perry, a list of physical task boards examples, https://agiletools.wordpress.com/2007/11/24/task-boards-telling-a-compelling-agile-story/

Any issue that could slow down a team's progress will affect the team and keep them from remaining focused during the iteration. That's why it's extremely important to teach the team ways to identify, raise and remove impediments. Here some techniques that could help you to help your teams deal with impediments:

Identifying, raising and removing

During the daily sync, invite team members to share what's blocking them from getting the work done that the team committed to do at the iteration planning. Given that as the Scrum Master, one of my responsibilities is to remove impediments along the way that are preventing the team from reaching the iteration goal; I ask them for permission to add a section to the team's physical task board, where we can track impediments during the iteration. Depending on the team, and how many people are in the team, this technique could be really useful to help the team not only in identifying the impediments but also to raising and removing them.

Visually the impediments section within the team's physical task board looks like the personal Kanban displayed in the picture that follows:

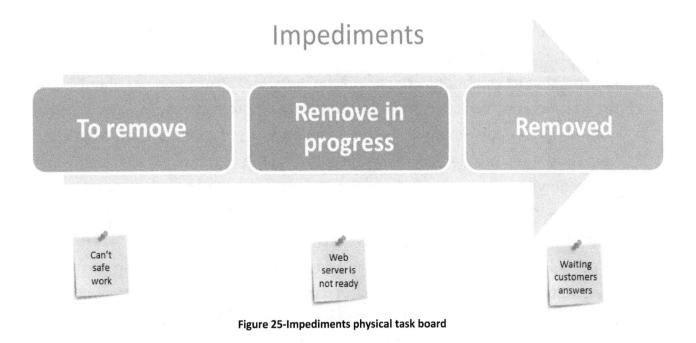

Figure 25-Impediments physical task board

Removing

When removing impediments, I've often seen in the field that there is confusion about who should do it, given that it's explicitly part of the Scrum Master's Job Description. I prefer to share that responsibility with the team using this approach:

"Team identifies & raise impediments **=> team member tries to remove impediment => if not possible then=> Team member and Scrum Master try together to remove impediment=> If not possible then => Scrum Master ask for Product Owner's help to try to remove impediment => If not possible then =>** Scrum Master scales impediment until it gets removed"

How to deal with interruptions

It's a fact that the team will be faced with interruptions during the iteration, and if you accept that, then life will be easier, and the team will be able to set some rules to deal with them. I prefer to be flexible and let the team decide how to deal with interruptions. There are several ways that I've found that work to help the team stay focused even when interrupted:

- The first time that an interruption hits the team, take it as it is, let it flow, take some notes and then invite the team to reflect about it. Make it visible and acknowledge the fact that interruptions are part of the work life. I like to reflect about it during the iteration retrospective, at a time and place where the team can decide what to do and agree upon what will be the team's process to manage interruptions the next time. Keep this decision as visible as possible, so that everyone outside of the team knows how the team will manage interruptions. Please discuss what the team means by interruptions and try to get consensus of the meaning, in order to avoid confusion when collaborating.

- I like to keep track of interruptions and make them visible during the iteration review (iteration status). Additionally, I would mention them in the iteration report once the iteration is done. This would serve you and the team for several purposes. For example, it would create awareness if the interruptions ever become extra work that could rule the team's iterations. If the Product Owner is taking advantage of it, you could use the iteration report and the interruption chart trends as facts to support your discussions with the Product Owner and to reflect together with the team during the iteration retrospective if, in any case, the interruptions become an issue that impedes the team's progress.

- Create the habit to collaborate and tackle interruptions together. I would suggest that the Product Owners talk directly with the Development Team to decide together how a particular interruption will be managed.
- From your point of view, when the decision is too risky, challenge the agile team by asking open ended questions to validate and reinforce their decisions and how the interruption will be managed this time around.

Pay attention to people's dysfunctional behaviors during the iteration

Your instincts are the most important tools when working with people, especially during the forming stage of the team's journey. **Leanne Howard**[18] has identified three areas to look for when trying to identify dysfunction in a team:

- **Lack of communication** - when team members aren't voicing their opinions or collaborating.
- **Lack of participation** - when the whole team isn't getting involved in key ceremonies.
- **Lack of cooperation** - when there remains segregation between traditional roles.
- I would add, **Lack of trust** – when team members are not genuinely open with one another about their mistakes and weaknesses and have issues being vulnerable in front of the team.

Some signs of dysfunctional behavior will be visible during activities where collaboration and communication are required to move forward and make progress to continue improving. Daily Sync Meetings, Product Backlog Refinements, Iteration Reviews and Iteration Retrospectives are activities where people's dysfunctional behaviors could be identified. Here some examples of potential red flags that could get in the way of the team staying focused during the iteration:

Lack of communication

- People on their phones, tablets, or computers without paying attention to others.
- The 'war room' of the team is quiet, too quiet; it seems that nothing is going on.
- People's attitudes that would affect others when participating.

Lack of participation

- People frequently arriving late to team meetings after agreeing to behave differently.
- People not wanting to talk or share their ideas/opinions with the group.

Lack of cooperation

- People acting weird, like trying to distract the group if they have the opportunity.
- People that are showing laziness during meetings, they seem to be disengaged.

Lack of trust

- People afraid of sharing their code with other team members, fearing judgement.
- People avoid raising impediments because that could lead to trouble with managers or other people within the organization.
- People making noises when others are talking, such as whispering, coughing, clearing their throat, etc.

What techniques should we use to deal with People's dysfunctional behavior?

Lack of communication

At the very beginning I like to introduce what is called "Alliance, Attitudes and Agreements"[19]. This flip chart represents the code of conduct or suggested behaviors that would be accepted by the team once in a meeting. What I do to introduce it to the team is this:

This flip chart represents the code of conduct or suggested behaviors that would be accepted by the team once in a meeting. What I do to introduce this to the team is:

During our first iteration retrospective I bring a flip chart with me that will have some suggested behavior already written on it that would ease the conversation and facilitate decision making. I like to start by saying "This instrument represents our alliance, attitudes and agreements as a team. It will help when collaborating, by establishing some rules that we will set together, in order to enable communication and engage into powerful and productive collaboration".

---

[19] Lyssa Adkins, "Alliance, Attitudes and Agreements", http://www.jesusmendez.ca/wp-content/uploads/2015/01/Code_of_Conduct_Alliance_Attitudes_Agreements-Strategies-for-dealing-with-dysfunctional-behavior-template.pdf

Once that's done, I invite the team to revise each written behavior and to confirm that we are willing to respect what we have agreed upon. Then I ask them to let me know how I can help the team stick to these alliances, attitudes and agreements; so that I can refer to that decision once the team has engaged to collaborate in a meeting and something written is not respected.

Lack of participation

I've learned by failing, that participation at meetings should be optional. A way to keep it optional, to create habits and empower the team to own their activities is to avoid forcing them to come. I know that what I'm saying here seems to go against the purpose of team collaboration, but this is where trust comes to the forefront; I trust you. So, here is my suggestion: **Let them go!**

How to do it?

- Avoid forcing them to come to their own meetings, instead take notes and please stick to the meeting agenda with the people that are there. Take notes to see if there are patterns with team members.
- Once they show up, please avoid saying annoying phrases, like "Finally here". Instead welcome them and please smile.
- Keep a check on the emotions that you experience, once people arrive late, or don't show up at all to meetings that you are facilitating. It could help you grow your self-awareness.
- Make meetings more fun by creating a safe atmosphere where people can do almost whatever they want. Don't be negative; this will work.
- If your patterns are confirmed, validate your perceptions with the team and once confirmed by the team, use facts to confront the person individually in an exploratory one-to-one conversation, where you would share what you have observed in the field and how that's impacting the team's progress.
- If one-to-one doesn't work, then be courageous and bring the point up for discussion at the next iteration retrospective and invite the team to share how the lack of participation is impacting team's progression.

Lack of cooperation

Something that I've learned from other experienced coaches like **Michel Céré**[20] is that when working with people, one of the best ways to help them to grow is to become their mirror. Mirroring other people's behaviors will reflect to them what is potentially invisible to their eyes and maybe will create some awareness that will lead to changing their ways when interacting and collaborating with others. That's what I would like to recommend when you face a lack of cooperation from someone in a team; make things visible to them first and then to the team.

Lack of trust

In reference to trust, we are talking about our main priority when forming agile teams. Building a team that trusts each other should remain our main goal; the big question here is **how to do that**?

A way to do it is to use one of the exercises from the book "Overcoming the Five Dysfunctions of a Team, a field guide"[21] written by **Patrick Lencioni**[22], called "Review of the Short-Form Team Assessment". What I've learned by doing this exercise is that there is a need to create a vision of the team that we aspire to become and that starts with trust; being able to talk about our weaknesses, recognize the weaknesses in us and be able to share them humbly. The things that are really difficult to teach but that are easily learned by modeling and copying. It's here, when being a role model and being the leader that they need, it becomes extremely important for them and that responsibility lies in your hands.

Here are some techniques to help you do that:

- Start all conversations with "We" instead of you/they.
- When you've made a mistake, show vulnerability in front of the team. Recognize your mistake and sincerely apologize for what you've done.
- Stick to your promises, do what you say and say what you do.
- Be consistent as much as you can with your work.

---

[20] Michel Cere, Software Development Director at Seedbox Technologies Inc., https://www.linkedin.com/in/michelcere/fr
[21] Patrick Lencioni, Overcoming The Five Dysfunctions of a Team, a field guide",
http://www.tablegroup.com/books/dysfunctions
[22] Patrick Lencioni, http://www.tablegroup.com/pat/

- Always, always show up on time for meetings, show that your caring is real.
- Be there to serve them, and to help them go through the team's journey together.
- Celebrate progress, learning from experience, but be truthful.
- It's all about them, not about you and how you feel.
- Respect their decisions and trust them because they know how to do it.
- Be truthful with yourself and stick to your personality by being authentic.
- Get yourself a coach that can help you increase self-awareness and raise your emotional intelligence skills.
- Say hello, answer people's questions and stick to the team's alliance, attitudes and agreements.
- Protect the team from outsiders and live with the consequences.
- Be humble to accept that human beings are unique and different and there is always something that you can learn from others.
- Show that you care, and do it from your heart, please avoid faking it.

> **Tip:** *"What if you take criticisms and blame as gifts? What would be different for you? What could you learn from it? What would be possible?"*
>
> **Mike Edwards & Jesus Mendez Coaching Sessions 2015**

The six (6) levels of Agile Planning

Inspired from **Russell Pannone's**[23] presentation called "**5 levels of agile planning explained simply**"[24] and the experiments that I've done in the field with several agile teams about agile planning. I've combined it all to show you what I've called **the six (6) levels of agile planning** as seen in the picture that follows:

6 Levels of Agile Planning

Level	Frequency	Main Roles	Outcome
Strategic Goal Setting	**1-2** times/year (*)	Stakeholder(s)	**Strategic Plan**
Product Road Map (Alignment)	**Every iteration**	Stakeholder(s) + Product Owner	Product Road Map Goals set
Team's Road map (Tactic goals)	**4** times/year (*) Updated Every Iteration	Product Owner + Dev.Team + SM	Team's Road Map + Upcoming iteration goal set
Product Backlog Refinement (Operational goals)	**Every iteration**	Product Owner + Dev.Team + SM	Upcoming Iteration goal content revised + Product Backlog Updated
Iteration Planning	**Every iteration**	Product Owner + Dev.Team + SM	Iteration backlog
Daily Planning	Every daily sync	Dev.Team	Iteration backlog updated

* Frecuency depends on Context

Figure 26- 6 Levels of Agile Planning

[23] Russell Pannone, https://www.linkedin.com/in/russellpannone
[24] Russell Pannone, "5 Levels of Agile Planning explained simply", http://www.slideshare.net/rpannone/5-levels-of-agile-planning-explained-simply

Ideal Scenario

Ideally our goal is to have the six (6) levels of agile product planning in place in the organization, so the teams can build what the Stakeholders think would bring more value to the business and its customers. The product vision would be implemented through the team's product road maps, which would drive the products that are developed by the team and would be inspected and adapted through the Product Road Map meetings. The Stakeholders and Product Owners would set tactical goals aligned with strategic organizational goals, to keep the team and product development closely aligned.

In this scenario, Stakeholders, Product Owners and Agile Teams are continuously collaborating to build a product that would solve customer problems and needs. This really sounds amazing but, how does this happen in real life? Is it possible? Let's navigate through a real example, to see how this ideal scenario has been implemented:

Strategic Goal Setting (High level plan for the year)

Company owners, members of the board and stakeholders would define strategic goals that the organization envisions will be achieved by the end of the fiscal year. In order to avoid changes and keep the organization focused, the strategic plan would be done at the beginning of the fiscal year, with a mid-year review to adjust direction based on the facts gathered at mid-year. For further references, take a look at the table below that I've created to give you a visual example of how I've set strategic goals for my own products next year.

Product Road Map (Alignment)

At this level of agile planning, stakeholders, with the product owners, would discuss, revise and update the priorities set at the strategic level, in order to enable the creation of the team's product road map. The Product Owner would have a clear picture about what goals the company is prepared to achieve in order to answer team questions; by when and why they are a priority. Every iteration the stakeholder and product owner would meet to revise and update the team's product road map once created.

Team's Product Road Map (Defining tactic goals)

At this level, the Product Owner assisted by the Scrum Master/Agile Coach creates the tactical goals that the agile team will achieve to help the organization reach the strategic goals previously set. Once created, the team's product road map would serve to facilitate product road map conversations between the stakeholder and the product owner. It would also create a bridge between the product developed by the agile team and the strategic goal set by the organization, which I've seen enables collaboration, accelerates time to market, and increases team happiness by increasing the stakeholder's satisfaction.

Product Backlog Refinement (Operational goals)

At this level of agile planning; once the tactical goals are set, it is time to discuss and plan with the team how to build each piece of the map, focusing mainly on what's next in the team's product road map and how long it's going to take to put the map together. At least once per iteration, the agile team will meet to refine the content of the Product Backlog, investing time on the things that are most important to the organization. It's at this level where the agile team would identify the operational goals that need to be reached to achieve the tactics defined in the team's product road map.

Iteration Planning

Once the iteration has started, the product owner brings to the team the iteration product wish list based on what was refined during the previous Product Backlog refinement meeting, as an input to facilitate iteration backlog creation.

Daily Planning

Every day, during the daily sync meeting, the agile team creates a daily plan where the iteration backlog will be updated with what the team has completed.

After going through the six (6) levels of agile planning shown above, what I want you to realize is the fact that no matter what scenario you and your teams are facing, you can put in place at least four (4) out of the six (6) levels of the agile planning model within your organization, without having to ask someone outside the organization to change anything

Strategic Goals

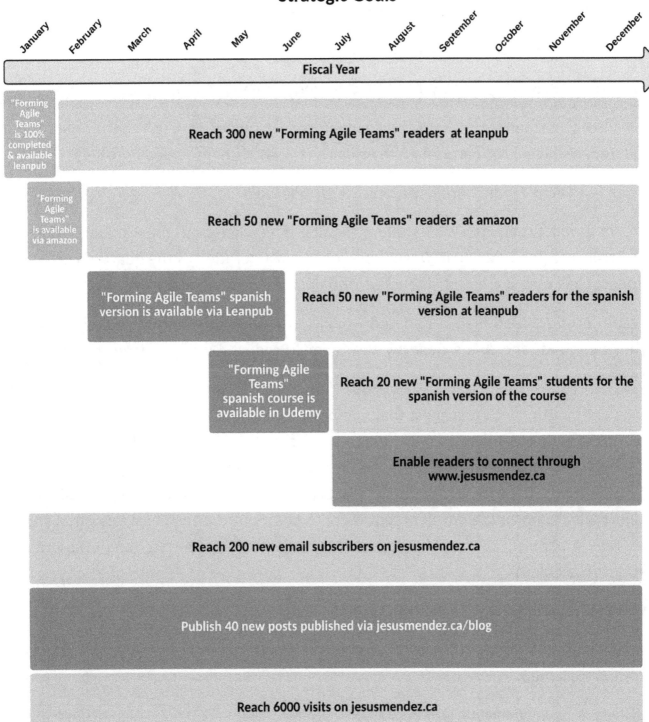

Figure 27- Product Planning Strategic Goals Example

Team's Product Road Map

What is a Team Product Road Map all about?

It's a **collaboration tool** created to plan the product road map for a specific team.

It is also a mechanism to help the team's product owner to keep the product vision updated, visible and at hand when revising its content or negotiating priorities.

When is a Team Product Road Map created/updated?

A team product road map is created for the first time when both the Product Owner and the Scrum Master agree on it. Once there, on the last iteration of the quarter a new team product road map is created, discussed, and updated by the agile team.

A team product road map is updated weekly, bi-weekly or monthly depending on the team's context, and that's done by the team's Product Owner assisted by the Scrum Master.

Once per month, I would suggest that you bring the product road map back to the team and go through it together. I have found that my favorite time to do this is at the beginning of the iteration planning, why? Because everybody's mind is fresh! So it's a great time to discuss what's happening regarding the product. I would also consider this as an opportunity to invite the development team to point out the technical tasks that should be done in parallel; to properly support the product evolution described in the team's product road map.

Who Creates/Updates A Team Product Road Map and How?

Here is what I've found that works well for each role when creating/updating a team product road map:

Role	Responsibilities
Scrum Master/Agile Coach	- Helps Product Owner with creating the Team's Product Road Map. - Teach/Coach Product Owner about the benefits of using the Team's Product Road Map. - Helps the Product Owner with keeping the Team's Product Road Map updated. - Inspects and adapts the Team's Product Road Map to the Team's context and the Product Owner's planning style.

Figure 28- Team's Product Road Map - Scrum Master/Agile Coach role and responsibilities

Role	Responsibilities
Scrum Master/Agile Coach	- Ensures that Product Owner keeps the Team's Product Road Map visible. - Invites Product Owner to gather, validate and negotiate goals with the Stakeholders recurrently. - Invites Product Owner to collaborate with the Development Team when updating the Team's Product Road Map. - Facilitates interactions between the Stakeholders, the Product Owner and the Development Team about planning the product. - Encourages continuous improvement by setting regular meetings with the Product Owner to follow up with the Team's Product Road Map. - Helps Product Owner with planning product backlog refinement content ahead. - Eases product planning process by setting a Team Product Road Map. - Coach Agile Team with instilling a high-level abstract thinking mindset for product planning.

Figure 29- Team's Product Road Map - Scrum Master/Agile Coach role and responsibilities

Role	Responsibilities
Stakeholder(s)	- Sets Product Road Map high level (Division/Organization) goals. - Coaches the Product Owner about the Team's Product Road Map priority settings. - Answers questions about product vision, strategic goals and budget for product development. - Empowers the Product Owner to prioritize the Team's Product Road Map. - Collaborates with the Agile Team during Product Backlog Refinement discovery sessions. - Facilitates product planning by providing clear goals and setting feasible priorities. - Eases Product Owner job by providing achievable high-level goals. - Provides recurrent feedback to the Product Owner about the Team's Product Road Map. - Helps the Product Owner set Product Vision. - Keeps the Product Owner focused on what will bring value to the organization. - Collaborates with Scrum Master/Agile Coach by removing impediments in the way of the Team's Product Road Map creation/update.

Figure 30- Team's Product Road Map - Stakeholder(s) role and responsibilities

Role	Responsibilities
Development Team	- Challenge the Team's Product Road Map content by asking questions to the Product Owner. - Provides technological advice to support the Team's Product Road Map. - Interacts with the Product Owner and the Stakeholder(s) to enrich Product Backlog refinement discovery sessions.

Figure 31-Team's Product Road Map - Development Team role and responsibilities

Role	Responsibilities
Development Team	- Collaborates with the Product Owner and the Scrum Master/Agile Coach when building or updating the Team's Product Road Map. - Makes technological requirements visible to the Agile Team. - Participates actively on Product Backlog Refinements sessions to keep product plans.

Figure 32-Team's Product Road Map - Development Team role and responsibilities

Role	Responsibilities
Line Manager(s)	- Supports the Team's Product Road Map process. - Challenges the Agile Team on technical aspects of the Team's Product Road Map. - Collaborates with the Scrum Master/Agile Coach by removing impediments in the way of the Team's Product Road Map creation/update.

Figure 33-Team's Product Road Map - Line Manager Responsibilities

Role	Responsibilities
Product Owner	- Creates the Team's Product Road Map. - Gathers the Team's Product Road Map content from the Stakeholders. - Sets the Team's Product Road Map goals using business values or provides necessary information which could help supports its decisions. - Negotiates the Team's Product Road Map goals priorities. - Establishes the ideal dates of the Team's Product Road Map goals. - Makes the Team's Product Road Map visible to the Development Team and the rest of the organization. - Keeps the Team's Product Road Map updated. - Sets the Team's Product Road Map upcoming iteration goal. - Discusses the Team's Product Road Map content with the Agile Team. - Encourages collaboration between the Stakeholders and the Development Team about the future of the product. - Collaborates with the Scrum Master/Agile Coach to keep the Team's Product Road Map updated.

Figure 34-Team's Product Road Map - Product Owner Responsibilities

Let's go through the team's product road map template that I've created; sharing with you some techniques to go through this crucial step of agile planning:

Team's Product Road Map Template – Overview

Suggested Steps	
Purpose	**Techniques**
STEP 1 – Identify Goals	
Invite the Product Owner to answer the following question: What do we want to achieve in terms of the product within the next quarter (3 months)?	• Once the Product Owner has accepted its willingness to try out the tool, use an empty flip chart to draw the main elements of the Team's Product Road map template on it. • Invite the Product Owner to answer the question: What do we want to achieve in terms of the Product within the next Quarter (Three months)
STEP 2 – Set Goals and Ideal Dates	
Transform each given answer into a Goal. Then write it down in a post it.	• Write down a goal per post-it and then stick it into the flip chart, below the area called "Goals". **Tip:** Keep in mind that this template is a tool to start talking about product goals, with an abstraction level that would allow business to be able to maneuver. So, avoid forcing it. Instead, invite the product team to explore it as an option to keep the team in sync with what the business wants, and present it as visual aide to facilitate stakeholder management.
STEP 3 – Identify Project(s) The Team Will Focus On (Optional)	
Identify with the Product Owner those projects that the agile team will be focusing on during the Quarter and create a post it for each one of them.	• Once goals have been set, I love to invite the Product Owner to identify the projects that we (the team) would be focusing on during the upcoming three months. Remember, the goal here is to engage in a high-level conversation, so please keep it simple. Remember to add a post-it per project to the flip team's product road map flip chart project area. • Now is time to discuss about Ideal dates per goal. Why to do that? It would give the agile team an idea about priorities. It would also help the team to organize how things are going to be developed and delivered then. It's really up to you to decide the way to go at this stage of the process. I like to go over and over again, until all goals have an ideal date set.

STEP 4 – Forecast Upcoming Iteration Goal

Based on the defined Goals, invite the Product Owner to forecast the upcoming Iteration Goal	• Once product road map goals are set and ideal dates have been identified, what's the main thing to tackle in the upcoming iteration should be clear. At this point of the conversation, I like to invite the Product Owner to answer the following question: What's the main thing you want the team achieves by the end of the upcoming iteration, based on the goals and projects already set? Having this question answered, you would have helped the agile team with:
	
	    ○ Forecast upcoming Iteration goal
	    ○ Get set for upcoming Product Backlog Refinement sessions
	    ○ Ease next iteration planning by having the team focused on what has been discussed, and in sync with what the business wants.
	
	Tip: Encourage Product Owners to share Team's Product Road map assumptions and conclusions with stakeholders frequently, in order to keep priorities synchronized, increase collaboration and reduce waste. It's recommended that at least once per iteration, a meeting occurs to collaborate about the subject.

STEP 5 – Make the Plan Visible

Make it visible for the team	• Be sure that the Product Owner feels comfortable to share the created "Team's Product Road Map" with the team. Then identify together when the most appropriate time would be to make it visible to the team. **Tip:** If you both decide to make it visible to the development team, I would recommend inviting them to make the final decision where to make it visible. If there are questions concerning the visibility of the product road map, then invite the Product Owner to share briefly what it's about and then set a meeting together to go through its content.

STEP 6 – Shared Understanding	
Look for shared understanding Product Owner + Development Team	Once a Team's Product Road Map is created, and is place in the team's war room, it's time to go through its content together.

Set a meeting to do that. For me personally, I like to do it at the beginning of the iteration planning. If so, remember to ask the team's permission to do it then. Then explain the purpose behind the new product road map and what's in it for the development team and get ready to facilitate the conversation between the development team and the Product Owner.

Tip: Observe people's reactions; look for dysfunctional behavior that could compromise collaboration.

The main goal here is for the agile team to share understanding about the proposed goals identified by the Product Owner in the Team's Product Road Map for the next quarter.

How to do it?
First, invite the Product Owner to explain each goal by sharing:
- What the goal is about.
- Business reasons to do it during the next quarter.
- Any additional detail that could help the development team to understand what's needed.

Then, invite the team to challenge the Product Owner's goals by asking questions to clarify the high-level scope.

Tip: Remind the team that what has been presented is a high-level goal, so further discussions will happen in the Product Backlog Refinements sessions; to get detailed technological clarifications.

Now, invite the development team to identify some technological goals that need to be reached, in order to support the proposed business goals. I'm talking about new technologies that need to be put in place, new servers or training that maybe the development team would require to properly do what the business needs.

How to do it?
First, go through each of the team's product road map goals previously identified by the Product Owner and then invite the development team to:
- Identify any technological gap that could impede reaching the goals.
- Set one technical goal per business goal if there is one. |

	• Explain high level, what does the team need to achieve and why is this required to reach the business goal. Once the discussion is done, confirm that everyone is satisfied with the outcome and celebrate that the team has created the team's first product road map
STEP 7 – Set Rhythm	
Define the rhythm to keep team's road map updated	Once the agile team is on the same page, invite the Product Owner to help you keep him/her accountable by sustaining the content of the team's product road map with frequent updates. **For Updates** I like to do it at least once per iteration with the Product Owner and once per two iterations with the development team. A good practice is to invite the team to decide the frequency that best suits their needs. I like to bring the Team's Product Road Map to the team's iteration planning and to some Product Backlog Refinement sessions, in order to keep the conversation, open more often. **A new Quarter** For the quarterly version, I would meet once with the Product Owner, during the previous iteration before the new quarter starts and then once with the whole agile team, to go through it together.

Figure 35- Team's Product Road Map Template Overview – Summary Part A

Instructions - Part A

How to set it up

1. On an empty flip chart (my favorite wall pad is the 3M Self-Stick Wall Pad, 2 x 20, 20 x 23 inches) write **at the center-top "Team's Product Road Map" as the title**, using your preferred marker.

2. Just below the title, please write down the word "Goals" as the subtitle.

3. Using two (2) 3 x 3 inch post-its, place them one below the other, below the **subtitle "Goals"** and use a ruler to trace a straight line from the right to left end of the flip chart, which would be used as a time line during the quarter.

4. Divide the straight line in three (3) sections about the same size.

5. To **identify the months** of the quarter, on a sticky note (I like to use 3 x 3 inches 3M post-its) write down the name of the upcoming three months, one month per sticky note.

6. Stick each note in ascending order over the straight line, right in the middle of one of three areas.

7. **To identify the iterations** over the straight line, on a sticky note (I like to use 2 x 1.5 inches 3M post-its) write down "Iteration 1". Stick the note at the beginning of the straight line on the left side of the flip chart. Repeat this step, horizontally until you reach the sticky note with "Iteration 6". I like to use two iterations per month. But that really depends of how long iterations are with your content.

8. **(Optional) If you want to add projects. To identify them -** on a sticky note (I like to use 2 x 1.5 inches 3M post-its) write down the name of the project and then stick the note just below the beginning of the straight line on the left side of the flip chart. Repeat this step vertical until you have added the last project.

Instructions - Part B

How to fill it up

1. **Goals -** Invite the Product Owner to answer the question: What do we want to achieve in terms of the product within the next quarter (Three months)? Then write down a goal per post-it and stick it onto the flip chart, below the zone called "Goals".

2. **Projects (Optional) -** Invite the Product Owner to answer the question: What projects will the team focus on within the next quarter (Three months)? Then write down a project per post-it and stick it onto the flip chart vertically, below the very beginning of the straight timeline.

3. **Upcoming Iteration Goal -** Based on the goals defined by the Product Owner, only when step 6 of the Team's Product Road Map is done, invite the Product Owner to forecast an upcoming iteration goal and write it down on a sticky note (I like to use 3 x 3 inches 3M post-its). Stick the iteration goal right below the associated iteration on the flip chart.

4. **Have fun!**

Visual Instructions

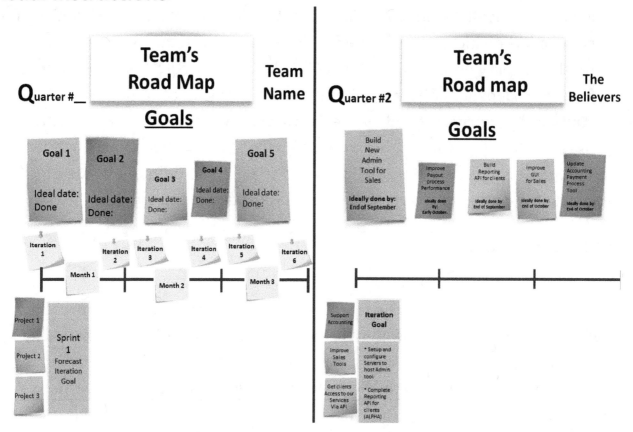

Figure 36- Team's Product Road Map Template- Visual Instruction

Simple Explanation

✔	Main Steps	WHY
	Identify Goals	• Adds enough visibility to what would be done by the team next. • Enables required conversations to connect strategic goals with tactical goals. • Helps identify needs & potential problems ahead. • Creates the planning mindset for the team. • Engages Product Owner to invest time in defining achievable goals. • Enables collaboration and increases inspection and adaption based on concrete things.

✔	Main Steps	WHY
	Set Goals And Ideal Dates	• Helps with setting expectations in terms of feasibility. • Enables conversation and collaboration within the agile team.
	Identify Project(s) The Team Will Focus On	• Increases visibility about the projects that the team would be working on during the next quarter. • Helps Product Owner collaborates with stakeholders when negotiating priorities. • Creates team awareness to deal with context shifting.
	Forecast Upcoming Iteration Goal	• Increases the capacity of the team to focus just in what's important now. • Reduces waste in no valuable conversations about things that won't be don't at the moment. • Helps Product Owner with keeping the development team refining only what's going to be develop in the upcoming iteration.
	Make the Plan Visible	• Adds some transparency and visibility to what's next in the Product/Service pipeline. • Enforce team self-organization and ownership of the space.
	Share Understanding	• Helps team's conversation about what's next. • Gets the team a chance to collaborate towards a common purpose. • Helps with mitigating potential risks ahead. • Engages team members with what's coming.
	Set the Rhythm	• Enables the team to set the habit to plan the product ahead. • Keep the team accountable about its own future.

Figure 37- Team's Product Road Map Template- Simple Explanation

6. Iteration Product Backlog Refinement

What is the Iteration Product Backlog Refinement About?

The Product Backlog refinement is considered as "the act of adding detail, estimates, and order to items in the Product Backlog" within the Scrum guide[25]

When is the Iteration Product Backlog Refinement Held?

It really depends; given that it's considered as "an ongoing process in which the Product Owner and the Development Team collaborate on the details of Product Backlog items"; technically it could be called whenever the Scrum Team decides it is required during the sprint.

In my experience, I prefer to keep it as a fixed act within the sprint; I mean at the same time and place, in order to facilitate that it becomes a habit for the team.

Who Participates in the Product Backlog Refinement and How?

Here is what I've found works better for each role during participation in the Product Backlog refinement:

Role	Responsibilities
Product Owner	- Ensures that Product Backlog items or the idea/proposal to be discussed is ready to be revealed to the team. • To me, ready to be discussed means that: ○ The "What" and "Why" questions are able to be answered. ○ Acceptance criteria have been established for each Product Backlog item. - Explains what the goal of the session is (give some context to the audience). • If its goal is to refine ideas, proposals and help Stakeholders and Product Owners scope potential projects with the Development Team, we would go for what I've called a "Discovery session". In this type of Product Backlog refinement, high level estimation could happen but rarely at the User Story/Task level. ○ The Product Owner invites key Stakeholders to collaborate by participating in the meeting. - Encourages collaboration between the stakeholders and the development team.

Figure 38- Iteration Product Backlog Refinement - Product Owner role and responsibilities

---

[25] Scrum Guide, http://www.scrumguides.org/scrum-guide.html

Role	Responsibilities
Product Owner	- Explains what the goal of the session is (give some context to the audience). • **Frequent Iteration Product Backlog refinement** where, User Stories have already been sliced by the Scrum Team and common understanding is required in order to estimate the effort required to get it done; and where risks, complexity, dependencies and other related details need further discussion within the team. - Exposes the business perspective of each idea/Product Backlog item to the Development Team, referring specifically to: • What needs to be done? • Why are we discussing it now? • Answers questions about business rules, product or project constraints that could change the scope of the item that's being discussed. • Describe the conditions that need to be validated to consider the item complete, using the acceptance criteria discussed and agreed upon with the Development Team.

Figure 39- Iteration Product Backlog Refinement - Product Owner role and responsibilities

Role	Responsibilities
Development Team	- Collaborates with the Scrum Team by discussing openly "How" the discussed Product Backlog item would be approached. - When discussing the "How To" do things, I strongly recommend keeping it high level. Remember that what matters is to reach a common understanding about the high-level approach, so try to keep discussions at the strategic level. - Respectfully challenges the Product Owner/Stakeholders by asking questions to clarify "What" should be done and "Why" now. - Stays alert, open minded and ready to share other opinions. - Listening carefully to what others have to say. - Makes a strong effort to make get the Product Backlog refined.

Figure 40- Iteration Product Backlog Refinement - Development Team role and responsibilities

Role	Responsibilities
Stakeholder(s)	- Its presence is optional. - Answers Scrum Team questions. - Reinforces Product Owner's product/project vision. - Encourages continuous improvement mindset by giving direct feedback to the Scrum Team. - Challenges the Development Team by asking open ended questions regarding the potential solutions to its ideas/proposals. - Collaborates with the Scrum Master to create a safe environment to increase collaboration, visibility and transparency.

Figure 41- Iteration Product Backlog Refinement - Stakeholder(s) role and responsibilities

Role	Responsibilities
Specialist(s)	- Same responsibilities as the Development Team but I haven't often seen these people challenging the "What" and the "Why". What I've seen instead, is having them answer specific technical questions to clarify system related requirements.

Figure 42-Iteration Product Backlog Refinement - Specialist(s) role and responsibilities

Role	Responsibilities
Scrum Master/Agile Coach	- Ensures that the process happens at the same time and at the same place after agreement with the team. - Facilitates collaboration between the Development Team, the Product Owner and the Stakeholders. - Creates a safe environment to encompass the event and empowers collaboration. - Ensures that the meeting is structured and stays focused. - Identifies potential issues that are required to be addressed later and asks for responsible person (s) before the meeting ends. - Ensure that meeting stays within established time frame. - Challenges the "What" and the "Why" by asking open questions. - Helps the Scrum Team to go over the Product Backlog items as fast as is possible for the team, ensuring that the team is not stuck. - Teach/Coach the Scrum Team alternatives for estimating the project. • I like to show **some techniques**[26] to the team in a special workshop session that would help us get common understanding of what the process is about, why the Scrum Team does estimates and how it does it. - Teach/Coach the team techniques to improve the quality of the Product Backlog. • I like to explain at high level how a user story is created and what are good **acceptance criteria**[27]. - Verifies how the Product Backlog refinement act could be improved by asking the Scrum team.

Figure 43-Iteration Product Backlog Refinement - Scrum Master/Agile Coach role and responsibilities

What techniques could be used to getting the best out of the Product Backlog refinement?

<u>**Recurring weekly meetings with the Product Owner**</u> could be really helpful when getting ready for the Product Backlog refinement. Depending on how mature the Product Owner is, in terms of managing the content of its Product Backlog; it would require more involvement or less from the Scrum Master.

---

[26] Jesus Mendez, Product Backlog Item Estimation Techniques, http://www.jesusmendez.ca/wp-content/uploads/2014/01/Estimation-Techniques-Workshop-by-JM.pdf
[27] User Stories and acceptance criteria, http://blog.mimacom.com/user-stories-and-acceptance-criteria/

A Product Planning weekly meeting is a short meeting (in a two-week based sprint, it takes less than (1) hour) where the Scrum Master meets the Product Owner to collaborate about:

Timeline of the Product Plan

I like to start the conversation by asking some powerful questions about the product, for example: Where are we with the product? What are the goals? Where are we with the product goals (on or off track)? What's next in the Product pipeline and what does he/she need the team to do to get done? Moving on to next in the pipeline: when does he/she think it makes sense to start discussing about it with the Development Team and with the stakeholders? Is there anything that needs to be added or removed from the Product roadmap?

Assess Potential Risks

Based on the answers gathered in the previous step, I like to take the time to spot potential risks that could impact the team and the product. At this point of the conversation, if you get under the impression that something is off, please invite the Product Owner to discuss about it and to collaborate with you with finding possible ways to make the issue visible for the development team.

How do we assess risks?

There is a tool called "Risk management assessment for scrum teams ", that I've learned from **Cathy Axais**[28]; which would help a Scrum team decide what to do with a potential risk. It combines the potential risk impact level (low, medium or high) to identify in what way the issue could potentially affect the product, with the likelihood (low, medium or high) that the issue could happen.

Share Opinions, Issues and Ideas regarding the agile Team

What's that? Every single occasion that you have to collaborate and discuss with the Product Owner about how the team is doing; take it and say thank you, because it would be a sign that you're in the right track to get your Product Owner's heart, which will lead him/her to trust you. So, keep it up!

---

[28] Cathy Axais, Software Development Manager, Seedbox Technologies Inc.,https://www.linkedin.com/in/cathy-axais-a955b958

Why? I've noticed that having a closer relationship with the Product Owner has had a positive impact on the team's performance. So, any chance for reinforcing the relationship of trust, I'm totally in.

Offer your help

Ask the Product Owner what else you can do to help him/her excel owing his/her Product. Be there to support the Product Owner's role and empower him/her to become a leader for the team. I love to see it this way:

More help accepted => more trust established => higher collaboration=> Incredible results

Give and take Feedback

Don't be shy about asking how the Product Owner thinks you're doing and what points needs some improvement. Call for action and become vulnerable and you'll get to the point where he/she will ask your feedback as well. Remember, the Product Owner is your best ally, and your goal is to collaborate towards getting incredible results.

Other techniques

The **Team's Product Road Map template**[29] helps Scrum Masters/Agile Coaches help Product Owners to get the content of the upcoming Product Backlog refinement ready and in line with the Product Roadmap.

Another thing that I like using to help the team to improve and take ownership of keeping the Product Backlog updates is this: After the 5th time after my first the Product Backlog refinement session with a new team, I like to abstain from the meeting, so the team can figure things out on their own. **Let it go, observe how it goes and take notes to learn from the team habits, and then ask permission to share what've noticed with then.** Trust me; you would be surprised about the outcome!

And last but not least, please remember to **repeat, repeat and repeat.** I've learned, by practicing over and over again, that repetition gets people used to doing things and quite often ends up with these people incorporating these practices as part of their own lives.

---

[29] Jesus Mendez, "Team's Product Road Map template", http://www.jesusmendez.ca/wp-content/uploads/2015/10/Jesuss-Team-Roadmap-Template-V2.pdf

7. Iteration Review

What is the iteration Review for?

It's the event held to inspect what was done for the customer during the iteration and to adapt the Product Backlog if needed.

When is the iteration Review held?

It's held at the end of the iteration.

Who participates in the iteration Review and how?

Here is what I've found that works better for each role when participating in the iteration review:

Role	Responsibilities
Product Owner	- Invites key Stakeholders to collaborate by participating in the meeting. - Explains what the iteration goal was (give some context to the audience). - Discloses high level results of the iteration in terms of: • Forecasted user stories; • Completed ("Done") user stories; • Number of unplanned items added to the iteration; • Number of bugs found; • Number of bugs fixed. - (If needed) Discloses high level project status in terms of: • Current completion status (%); • Projected completion date; • Amount of iterations left to completion. - Discloses and discusses what's next in terms of the product: • Potential capabilities. • Encourages collaboration between the stakeholders and the development team about the future of the product.

Figure 44- Iteration Review - Product Owner Responsibilities

Role	Responsibilities
Development Team	- Updates audience about the issues, risks and improvements found during the iteration and its progress (and if, in any case, things that are not "Done"). - Demonstrates pieces of software considered "Done". - Answers questions related to the iteration content and the challenges faced.

Figure 45- Iteration Review - Development Team Responsibilities

Role	Responsibilities
Scrum Master/Agile Coach	- Ensures that the event happens at the same time and by the end of the iteration. - Facilitates collaboration between the Development Team, the Product Owner and the Stakeholders. - Creates a safe environment to contain the event and empowers collaboration. - Ensures that the meeting is structured and stays focused. - Identify potential issues that are required to be addressed later and asks for responsible people before the meeting ends. - Ensures that the meeting stays within the established time frame.

Figure 46- Iteration Review - Scrum Master/Agile Coach Responsibilities

Role	Responsibilities
Stakeholder(s)	- It's present to give feedback to the Scrum team about the product and the iteration. - Challenges the Product Owner about project status and what's next in the Product Backlog. - Encourages continuous improvement mindset by giving direct feedback to the Scrum team. - Challenges the Development Team about what was completed during the iteration. - Collaborates with the Scrum Master with creating a safe environment to increase collaboration, visibility and transparency.

Figure 47- Iteration Review - Stakeholder(s) Responsibilities

What other techniques could be used to improving the Iteration review?

<u>**Recurrent dry run meetings**</u> could be really helpful when getting ready for the iteration review. A dry run is a short meeting (for two-week iteration, it takes less than (1) hour) where the Agile team meets to identify:

<u>**What's "Done"? How?**</u>

The Development Team will review, item by item, within the Iteration Backlog to show the Product Owner which acceptance criteria is done (If it wasn't done previously during the iteration).

<u>**From what's "Done"**</u>

Pick and choose the most important items to be demonstrated, based on what was defined in the Iteration goal. Why pick and choose? Depending on the audience, if the development team goes through everything that was done during the iteration, instead of the 'pick and choose' criteria, sometimes the iteration review could be impacted in different ways.

Quick Updates

What's that?

All iteration backlog items considered not "Done" but whose progress is considerable enough that it's worthy to be demonstrated by the Development Team during the iteration review; in order to get feedback from the Stakeholders.

Why?

I've noticed that by not allowing the development team to present items considered not "Done" that they considered ready to be demonstrated, I was diminishing the power of short development cycles and feedback loops. Also, it was causing frustration in the development team up to a point that it was generating a negative impact.

Some results after several try outs

By doing this we showed the team what it means to add visibility and to be transparent when practicing Scrum; in addition to encouraging them to explain and get things done before the end of the iteration.

What's next?

Ask the Product Owner to list everything that he/she considers will be part of the focus of the next iteration. It could be as simple as showing the next iteration goal and high level content to launch the conversation with the Stakeholders that would be present during the iteration review.

Iteration Review Templates

Use **the iteration review template** to help you when making preparations for facilitating, holding and tracking the iteration review.

Repeat, repeat and repeat

Keep using these techniques until the team starts to own them. Something that I often do is not attending the dry-run meetings on purpose, so the team can figure it out on their own. The first time it could be awkward for the team, but after that they will be able to get it.

Iteration Review Template – Overview

	1-Iteration Status	2-Things to Demo	3-Updates	4-What's next
I N S T R U C T I O N S	Invite the **Product Owner to** complete the section(s) listed below with the values available at the moment. **Project Status:** What is the status of the project? Where we are in Terms of project completion? How much iteration left for Project completion? Is the project on track regarding the original baseline? **A - Project completion %** [Stories Completed/Stories forecasted]: **B - # Iterations left for completion:** **C- Projected on budget:** [Yes / No] **D - Project on track** [Yes / No] **Iteration Goal:** Why is it worthwhile to run the iteration? What should be achieved? For instance, address a risk, test an assumption, or deliver a feature. **Forecasted items [Story Points]:** **Completed (Done) items [Story Points]:** **Not (Done) items [List]:** **# Unplanned items (Injections):** **Bugs fixed/founded ratio:** **Test Coverage %:** **# Rollbacks:**	Invite the **Development Team** to list here everything that's considered "Done" by the Product Owner and will be demonstrated by the Development team during the Iteration review 5 Marble floor tiles ☑ 1 Gas hob ☑	Invite the **Development team to l**ist here all iteration backlog items considered not "Done" whose progress is considerable enough, that's worthy to be demonstrated by the Development team during the iteration review, in order to get feedback from the stakeholders. 5 Marble floor tiles ☑ 1 Gas hob 1 Gas hob	Invite the **Product Owner** to list here everything that he considered will be the iteration goal of the next iteration.
	2-Quick Updates			
		Invite the **Development Team** to list here everything that's considered "Done" by the Product Owner but just need a quick update. There is no Demonstration required		

	1-Iteration Status	2-Things to Demo	3-Updates	4-What's next
T I P S	**Keep it simple** Something that works for me, is to ask about those items available at the moment and be patient, the rest will come alone.	**Keeping track of the progress during the iteration review:** Something that works for me is showing that the iteration review is progressing by marking items from the list, once they are done. I do use markers or stickers to do that.	**Keeping track of the progress during the iteration review.** Something that works for me is showing that the iteration review is progressing by marking items from the list, once they are done. I do use markers or stickers to do that.	**Keep the communication open so then the Stakeholders can collaborate and exchange feedback to the Scrum Team** Something that had worked for me is to ask open ended questions once the Product Owner has presented the content of this section. Examples: • What do you think about what's next? • What about the priority? Is that accurate? • What else should we keep in consideration?

Figure 48 - Iteration Review Template overview

Instructions - Part A

During the Dry Run

1. Chose an empty board in the room where the iteration review would be held.

2. In a Super sticky note (I like 4 in x 4 in), right down the iteration review template suggested steps, one step sticky note.

3. Place all your super sticky notes in the board, one per column.

4. Filling the board, one column at a time:

   a. **Iteration Status**

      i. Invite the **Product Owner** to complete the section(s) **Project Status, Iteration Status** with the values available at the moment. For more details take a look to the **Iteration Status** section of the **Iteration Review Template – Overview**.

   b. **Things to Demo**

      i. Invite the **Development Team** to list here everything that's considered "**Done**" by the Product Owner and will be demonstrated by the Development team during the Iteration review.

      ii. Tip: Invite the team members to self-organize themselves by deciding who shows what.

   c. **Quick Update**

      i.   Invite the **Development Team** to list here, all iteration backlog items considered "**Done**" by the Product Owner and that the team considered important to share a quick update, in order to get feedback from the stakeholders.

d. Updates

      i.   Invite the **Development Team** to list here all iteration backlog items considered "**Not done**", whose progress is considerable enough, that's worthy to be demonstrated by the Development team during the iteration review, in order to get feedback from the stakeholders.

e. What's next

      i.   Invite the **Product Owner** to list here everything that he considered will be the iteration goal of the next iteration.

Instructions - Part B

During the Iteration Review

1. Remember that your role in this meeting is to facilitate it, so stick to it and give the team space to own it. Let them talk and be there to support their journey.
2. If there are new people in the room, I like to take time to explain what the purpose of the meeting is and how things are going to happen.
3. Keep track of the meeting progress. When facilitating, it's important to show that the meeting is progressing, that things are moving along. In order to help with it, I used to gray out the items that have been discussed in the board, once the discussion has completed.
4. Ask questions to get people's opinions and feedback for the team. I love asking permission to the audience before considering an issue done and grayed out for example.
5. Once the meeting is done, invite the people present in the room to share their perceptions about the Team's Performance Satisfaction, using a **Team's Performance Satisfaction template**[30].
6. Use Team's Performance Satisfaction results as an input to the iteration retrospective.
7. Have fun!

---

[30] Jesus Mendez, "Team's Performance Satisfaction Template", http://www.jesusmendez.ca/wp-content/uploads/2015/10/Jesuss-Team's-Performance-Satisfaction-Template-V2.pdf

Visual Instructions – Part 1

Dry Run Outcome

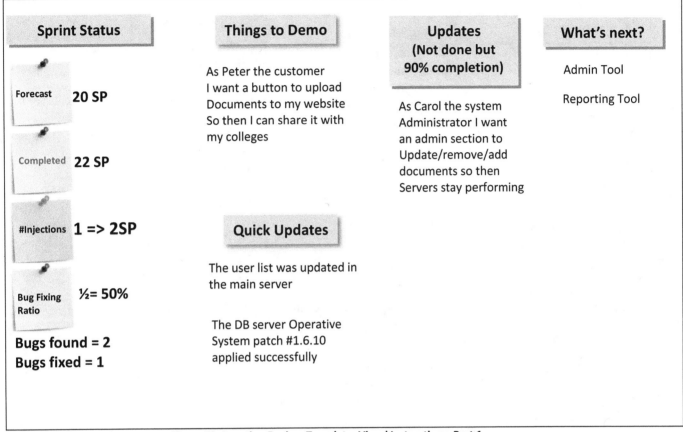

Figure 49- Iteration Review Template- Visual Instructions- Part 1

Visual Instructions – Part 2

During the meeting

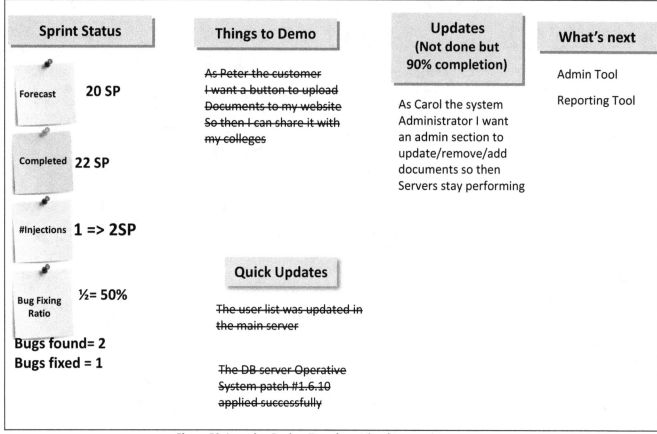

Figure 50- Iteration Review Template- Visual Instructions- Part 2

Simple Explanation

✔	Main Steps	WHY
	Iteration Status	• High level vision about what was done during the iteration • Helps with setting the stage properly for the next step (The demonstration)
	Things to Demo	• Gives visibility about what was done during the iteration. • Allows the team to get direct feedback the work that was done.
	Quick Updates	• Open the space for challenges and required conversations that would help the team to grow. • Encourage self-organization and team ownership. • Helps the team with taking responsibility about their work.
	Updates	• Helps the team to stay accountable and show things that are not done, but there is good progress. • Offers the opportunity to pivot early by saving time and changing the scope of things that are visible before getting it done. **Tip:** I would ask the team (PO) to agree upon what are the criteria for a task to be considered as a quick update. Personally, my teams are using tasks that are more than 80% completed.
	What's Next	• Adds some transparency and visibility to what's next in the Product/Service pipeline. • Opens the floor for Product Owners and the team to get challenged about what's next. • Offers the team a chance to demonstrate that everybody is in the same page or not.

Figure 51- Iteration Review Template- Simple Explanation

Detailed Explanation

✔	Main Steps	Techniques
	Iteration Status	• Prepare room by ensuring all artifacts are clear and visible prior to the meeting • Once the meeting has started invite the Product Owner to take the lead and present the content of the column to the audience. **Tip:** Coach the Product Owner to keep it short and high level, remember that the star of this event is the Development team.
	Things to Demo	• Once the Product Owner has completed introducing the Iteration Status, is time for the development team to shine and show the things that were decided to be demo during the Dry Run meeting. • Give the development team space to talk freely and own the presentation, by allowing them to speak. • Avoid interrupting them, and once they have finished presenting each feature, invite the people in the room to collaborate with the team by sharing them constructive feedback about what was demonstrated. • I like to gray out the feature in the board, as a visual sign that we are progressing with the meeting's agenda.
	Quick Updates	• Invite the development team to share with the audience, those Product Backlog Items considered "Done", which just require an update. No demonstration is required.
	Updates	• Invite the development team to make visible their progress about those things that were not completed within the iteration but are close to completion. • I like to invite my teams to share here, the Product Backlog item percentage of completion. That gives visibility to the audience and allows the team to get feedback during the early stages of their development process. I've notice that this helps with keeping team's motivation level elevated, because they feel that their efforts to get things done are worthy. • Invite people in the people to share their feedback with the teams and give space for conversations without losing the focus of the meeting.

Figure 52- Iteration Review Template- Detailed Explanation

Detailed Explanation (cont.)

✔	Main Steps	Techniques
	What's Next	• Invite the Product Owner to share what's next in the Product/Service pipeline. • Allow the Product Owner to talk freely. Giving space by listening carefully will give the Product Owner self-confidence to drive the Product and show the team that he/her owns it. • Start slowly closing the space. Observe when is the right time to intervene and invite people in the room to share their perceptions about the Team's Performance Satisfaction, using the **Team's Performance Satisfaction template.**

Team's Performance Satisfaction

What is the Team's Performance Satisfaction Template about?

The Team's Performance Satisfaction Template is a tool designed to collect people's opinion about their level of satisfaction of performance of a team during in a specific iteration.

When the Team's Performance Satisfaction Template is used?

It's meant to be used by the end of the iteration, after the iteration retrospective is over and before the next iteration is over. I prefer to keep it as a fixed event that occurs at the same time within the iteration, in order to turn it into a habit for the team.

What's the goal of the Team's Performance Satisfaction Template?

In my opinion, the main goal of the iteration retrospective is to create wisdom within the team by reflecting about the experiences to learn and continuously improve to get better results as soon as possible.

Instructions

By the end of the Iteration Review

1. Be sure that the Team's Performance Satisfaction Template is ready to be filled up, and that everybody in the room has a sticker ready to score the team.
2. Invite everybody in the room to share their opinions by rating their team satisfaction performance during the iteration that has ended.
3. Pay attention to get everyone participating by sharing its opinion through the board.
    a. If in any case, somebody doesn't want to share its opinion, let it go but then be curious to ask the reasons behind of it, you could be surprised.
4. If somebody scores 3 or less, I do ask the person to share verbally or at least write down in the post-it, what should be improved by the team to get a higher score next time.
5. Wait until everyone has expressed its opinion, and please remember: the team's opinion is really important. By exploring the reasons behind what the team has scored, you could get to undiscovered insights that could lead the team to figure potential issues.

6. Take a photo to keep track of it, it might be really useful to add visibility about how the team is being perceived within the company, increase team's moral, discover new perspectives, etc.

7. Keep the Team's Performance Satisfaction Template filled up and use it as an input to start the iteration retrospective.

8. Have fun!

Team's Performance Satisfaction Template - Overview

	Participant	Team Performance Satisfaction	Results
I N S T R U C T I O N S	At the end of the iteration review, the Scrum Master invites each participant to assess how they feel about the performance of the team during the iteration by sticking the post-it with their name on it, over the face that represents their feeling. Sam (SH) Jim (SH) Joe (PO) Jose (Dev) Lyn (Dev) Tim (SH) Mary (Dev) John (Dev) **Optional:** Only if the team ask for it the Scrum Master could share its impressions too Jesus (SM)	Team Performance Satisfaction — Score Very Happy — ⑤ Happy — ④ OK — ③ Sad — ② Very Sad — ①	Once the Iteration review is done and everybody have left the room, take a photo of the results, to use it when registering the results for further team performance reporting purposes. Once back in your desk, add each post it using the **value** assigned per each participant to each feeling. **Here is an example to help you calculate the "Team's Performance Satisfaction Score":** SAM = Very Happy => 5 Jim = Happy => 4 Joe = OK=> 3 Jose = Sad => 2 Mary = Happy => 4 Lyn = OK => 3 Tim = Very Sad =>1 Lyn and John were on vacation **TSS= (5 + 4 + 3 + 2 + 4 + 3 + 1) / 7 = 3.14, which** means that the overall perception was rated **OK**
T I P S	1 - Prepare Post-its before the iteration review starts. 2- You could also ask participants to write specific feedback in their own post-it		You could calculate the **TSS** per profile in order to identify issues, trends on it. For example, add up only stakeholders and then create a trend chart to keep track of stakeholder's perception.

Figure 53- Team's Performance Satisfaction Template - overview

Visual Instructions – Part 1

Before feedback is gathered

Figure 54- Team's Performance Satisfaction Template- Visual Instructions- Part 1

Visual Instructions – Part 2

After feedback is gathered

Figure 55- Team's Performance Satisfaction Template- Visual Instructions- Part 2

Simple Explanation

✔	Main Steps	WHY
	Invite People to Participate	• Enforces collaboration inside out the team. • Fosters conversations and set the foundations for required trust within the organization. • Fosters transparency and adds visibility to what the team is doing. • Allows people to share opinions and removes organizational barriers
	Pay Attention to What's Being Said Or Not	• Shows that you and the team care about others opinion.
	Keep Track of The Results Gathered	• In order to keep the mechanism a live, keep track of what's being said or not, would show them you care and that the feedback gathered is being used to doing something.
	Take Results to The Next Level	• Helps with improving teams moral. • Helps with improving how the team is perceived. • Fosters trust and collaboration inside out the organization. • Invites possibilities.

Figure 56- Team's Performance Satisfaction Template- Simple Explanation

Detailed Explanation

✔	Main Steps	Techniques
	Invite People to Participate	At the beginning of the Iteration Planning and every time that a new participant joins the iteration review, take time to explain the reasons behind using this artifact to gather feedback. It will help them to share their opinions and be open to collaborate. Remember that this is an invitation, so be patient and let the people opt in and participate just when they want to. Repeat, repeat and repeat until iteration review participants get familiar with the mechanism. Remember that what matters is not the artifact itself, is to get people collaborating and exchanging. Encourager feedback.

✔	Main Steps	Techniques
	Invite People to Participate	At the beginning of the Iteration Planning and every time that a new participant joins the iteration review, take time to explain the reasons behind using this artifact to gather feedback. It will help them to share their opinions and be open to collaborate. Remember that this is an invitation, so be patient and let the people opt in and participate just when they want to. Repeat, repeat and repeat until iteration review participants get familiar with the mechanism. Remember that what matters is not the artifact itself, is to get people collaborating and exchanging. Encourager feedback.
	Pay Attention to What's Being Said or Not	If somebody doesn't want to participate, let them go and then respectfully ask permission to hear the reasons behind that decision. Take care about what's being said through the artifact. I like to take a picture to the team's performance satisfaction template once has been completed, to further discussions with the team during the retrospective. I like also to do trend charts with Stakeholders results, and then make that information available to the team and then why not to the stakeholders.
	Keep Track of The Results Gathered	I like to do trend charts with Stakeholders results, and then make that information available to the team and then why not to the stakeholders. Keep track of the comments that people has made in the post-its and share them with the team during the iteration retrospective. Perhaps that could be used as input for a potential action item that would help the team improve. Remember that when forming a team, you are there to make things stick to their minds, so keep your notes up to date and gather collected comments for future interventions.
	Take Results to The Next Level	Use results to encourage the team to continue improving. I like to use the iteration report based on the Iteration Report Template, to discuss with the team how well or bad their performance has been perceived and what could be done in order to make the team better.

✔	Main Steps	Techniques
	Take Results to The Next Level	Celebrate learning often. I like to invite the team to get lunch together or just to get an ice cream when all stakeholders have scored Very Happy for example. Remember, what matters are that we are learning by experimenting. Do the same when people are Scoring, they are Very Sad. Stay positive.

Figure 57- Team's Performance Satisfaction - Detailed explanation

After a Team's Performance Satisfaction is filled, what's possible?

Once the iteration review is done and stakeholders, product owner and development team have expressed their level of team's performance satisfaction of the iteration, there are several possibilities and benefits of using gathered information. Here is what I've found has worked for me. I hope that together, we will increase the following list to use it as a reference in the community:

Possibility	Techniques	Benefits
Evaluate satisfaction per profile (Stakeholder, Product Owner, Development Team)	- Keep track of team performance satisfaction score per iteration and build some trend charts. - Bring trend charts to the team during next iteration retrospective and use it as a mechanism to encourage continuous improvement.	- Creates team's self-awareness about stakeholder's perceptions. - Enables new collaboration channels between stakeholders and agile team. - Enforce transparency and help with building trust by having open conversations. - Reduces team's fear to be exposed and evaluated. - Motivates team to raise results level iteration after iteration.
Possibility	**Techniques**	**Benefits**
Motivate the agile team to talk about results	Using the trend charts described above, invite the team to talk about it. I like to do that when	- Puts smiles on people faces.

	closing the iteration at the iteration planning, it is quite impressive how engaging it could be for the team to see how others perceive them, and how powerful it feels when your work is appreciated by the rest of the organization.	- Enables necessary conversations within the agile team about results. - Helps with taking out of the conversation, the commonly used phrase "But they said this or that about us" with facts that could be carried on. - Improves long term results. - Enables openness to be criticized and judged.

Figure 58-- Team's performance satisfaction- what's possible after

8. Iteration Retrospective

What is the iteration retrospective about?

The guys from **www.retrospective.com**[31] refer to retrospectives as a very old ritual used by human beings as a vehicle to discover, share and pass along learning from experience, sometimes called "wisdom". "A mechanism to look back or to move forward, something that every true learning organization has as part of its culture, and it's one of the best ways to grow - project by project - into a smarter and increasingly successful organization", "the collective telling of the story and mining the experience for wisdom" is how they refer to it.

Ben Linders[32] and **Luis Goncalves**[33] in their book, **Getting Value out of Agile Retrospectives**[34], define agile retrospectives as "a practice used by teams to reflect on their way of working and to become continuously better at what they do".

In my opinion, it is an opportunity to pause, reflect, analyze, and think collectively to learn and decide what and how to continue improving. It is a place for the team to grow hope and self-confidence. It's also a way to get away from bad habits, a way to face each other, a safe space to build self-awareness by practicing, and the heart of continuous improvement for any team willing to get out of the comfort zone to build greatness. It's one of my favorite "moments" during the iteration, where we can connect and get together to be energized to face the good and the bad.

When the iteration retrospective is held?

It's meant to happen by the end of the iteration, after the iteration review is over.
I prefer to keep it as a fixed event that occurs at the same time within the iteration, in order for it to become a habit for the team.

What's the goal of the iteration retrospective?

In my opinion, the main goal of the iteration retrospective is to create wisdom within the team by reflecting on the experiences to learn and to continuously improve by getting better results as soon as possible.

---

[31] Retrospective, http://www.retrospective.com/
[32] Ben Linders, http://www.benlinders.com/bio/
[33] Luis Goncalves, http://lmsgoncalves.com/about/
[34] Ben Linders, Luis Goncalves, Getting Value out of agile retrospectives, https://leanpub.com/gettingvalueoutofagileretrospectives

Who does participate in the iteration retrospective and how?

Here is what I've found to work better for each role when participating during the iteration retrospective:

Role	Responsibilities
Scrum Master/Agile coach	- Ensures that the act happens at the same time and at the same place after agreement with the team. - At this stage of the team's development, prepares and facilitates iteration retrospectives. - Enables collaboration between the Development Team and the Product Owner. - Creates a safe environment to contain the event and empowers collaboration. - Ensures that the meeting is structured and stays focused. - Helps team with identifying potential issues that are required to be addressed and ensures someone takes responsibility within the team before the meeting ends. - Ensures that meeting stays within established time frame. - Helps agile team to deliver results by challenging what happened during previous iterations and how that could be used to propel the team to better results. - Teaches/Coaches the team alternatives for keeping the meeting energized. - Teaches/Coaches the team techniques to improve the quality of the iteration retrospective. - Avoids judging others' opinions. - Keeps the team accountable by challenging different point of views. - Stays neutral and avoids taking things personal. - Encourages collaboration by setting the example. - Gets ready to rock and take the meeting to the next level.

Figure 59-Iteration Retrospective Scrum Master/Agile Coach role

Role	Responsibilities
Product Owner	- Industry says that the Product Owner's presence is optional but during the forming stage of the team's development process I would suggest that it is mandatory. - Supports Development Team's self-organization being transparent and making issues visible. - Collaborates with the Development Team and the Scrum Master/Agile Coach to get things done. - Challenge Development Team and the Scrum Master/Agile Coach points of view. - Collaborates with the Scrum Master/Agile Coach by respecting established meeting frequency and duration. - Propose actions to help the team continue improving.

Figure 60-Iteration Retrospective Product Owner role

Role	Responsibilities
Development team	- Shares responsibility with agile team about continuous improvement. - Stays alert, open minded and ready to listen to others. - Recognizes own faults and apologizes to others when needed. - Takes responsibility about things that should be done for the benefit of the agile team. - Gets ready to rock and take the meeting to the next level.

Figure 61- Iteration Retrospective Product Owner role

What techniques could be used to getting the best out of the iteration retrospective when forming an agile team?

1) **Pause.** I truly believe that when forming an agile team, we are forming leaders as well. That's why creating the need for pause through iteration retrospectives, is an amazing way to install the pause principle within the team. As Kevin Cashman refers to it in his book "The Pause Principle: Step back to lead forward", "The Pause principle is the conscious, intentional process of stepping back, within ourselves and outside of ourselves, to lead forward with greater authenticity, purpose, and contribution". That's what I'm looking for when forming an agile team, the team's soul, their own voice, what is that unique thing that will make stakeholders invest resources in it; that special ingredient that makes it different, inspiring.

2) **Be prepared and plan it.** I've noticed that there is a big difference between a well prepared retrospective and an improvised one. So please offer yourself and the team, the gift of being prepared in advance. By doing so, you will be sending several messages to the agile team:

    i. You've done your part, so you care about them.

    ii. There is some kind of plan in your mind to help them continue improving.

    iii. You respect them.

    b. **How to do it?** I have created the **iteration retrospective agenda**[35], to provide you with some ideas and inspiration on how to prepare and plan the agenda of your iteration retrospective. I invite you to ignite your creativity and free yourself by making your own version of it.

3) **Share intentions**. Once everyone is comfortably settled in the room and I sense people are ready to start, I wait in silence, with patience, for a clue that will show me that the

---

[35] For more details go to the "Tools and Exercise section" of the workbook

team is ready to listen to what I intend to do with the agenda that I'm about to propose to them.

a. **How to identify the clue?** Listen carefully and observe what's going on in the room. Wait with patience until there is almost no noise in the room. It is that specific moment when I will ask the team, are we ready to start? If the answer is positive, then is time to share what you intend to accomplish by the end of the retrospective. If the answer is negative, then I would ask the team, how much time is needed to start the meeting. If this is the case, I would pay attention to this behaviour and deal with it individually in a one on one session. In my experience, teams that are in the forming stage of their development process tend to show respect to the facilitator but occasionally they don't. If the clue is not evident, I will invite the team to start the meeting and then explore in future retrospectives, if this attitude becomes a pattern. It's rare but it could happen.

b. **Suggested attitude**. I prefer to wear my 'humble suit' when sharing intentions with the team. I would choose a voice tone that will transmit enthusiasm but control; I would smile and show that I feel confident about what we are going to do. I would also try to be transparent with what I'm capable of doing, and if there is something that I don't know I would tell them.

> **Tip:** Scrum Master/Agile Coach leadership skills will be fully exposed during iteration retrospectives. The team will examine and evaluate how good you are in your role. Given that, I would encourage you to pay attention to the tone of your voice when talking, your body language and the content that is being delivered. All that would be factored by the team as messages. So try to be clear, precise and straight to the point. Avoid confusion, stay calm and be yourself.

4) **Validate your agenda before starting**. Once your intentions have been shared, I would ask the team if there is another subject that should be discussed in priority. This question will open an opportunity to explore hidden subjects that could require immediate attention. It will also keep the **retrospective agenda**[36] flexible and add points to the relationship of trust that has been built.

---

[36] For more details go to the "Tools and Exercise section" of the workbook

5) **Breath.** Give yourself and the team a break to breathe and try as much as you can to do it together. Breathing is the process that moves air in and out of your body, it keeps organisms alive, and the team that we are forming here is a form of living organism, so let it breathe.

    a. How to do it? I like to ask the team about things that would make retrospectives more fun, and then try to get them, like a case of beer, candy and other simple stuff.

    b. Suggested attitude. I strongly recommend that you be authentic here, please don't force it but lead by example by allowing yourself to breathe. Take a seat and relax before starting the retrospective, put some music on or play with your favorite toy. Let yourself go, and you'll see how the team starts to copy your calmness and absorbs that state of mind.

6) **Be flexible but firm**. You will have only one unique chance to be part of the forming stage of the team that you're working with, so make it count. For that, I've found myself trying to guide the team's journey and trying to set my mark by telling them what to do and when. Please don't do that, instead I would invite you to be flexible and let the team begin their self-direction. Set the example, but open the space for craziness and joy. To make it worthwhile, celebrate different behaviors, laugh together, enjoy the moment and be there for them.

    a. **What about agile team members arriving late or showing up with a non-collaborative attitude?** I would love to tell you that I have an answer for that but I don't. My suggestion in this case would be to look ahead - beyond the dysfunctional behavior. Be curious and try to get that person's attention and have a talk about what you've observed. I strongly recommend you to go through this path if you have validated that the dysfunctional behavior is a pattern and that other people in the agile team have noticed it as well. Then take action by sharing your concerns directly with the person involved. But please remember, all this is new, not only for you but for the people in the team as well; so be flexible and continue observing, it could be that people just forgot.

7) **Keep the Team Cheerful**. Motivated people are open to learning, which leads to creativity and innovation. So be up for it and cheer them on, but pay close attention and please be authentic. Feel it, so you can inspire them to feel it too.

    a. **How to do it?** When forming an agile team, I focus on creating good habits by building solid structures that the team can use for the duration of the project.

One of those structures is arriving on time to meetings, so for those that do, I take time to congratulate them publicly in order to encourage that behavior within the full complement of the team. I like to focus retrospectives on positives and analyze results from a continual improvement perspective, so the team will get used to creating with positive thinking.

    b. **Suggested attitude.** Be genuine and connected with what happened during the iteration. Be compassionate with others, help to engage what matters to the team members and it will help you and the team to trust each other.

8) **Support improvement**. Invite the agile team to guide their destiny and own the space, by inspiring them with open ended questions like: what do you think we could do better? What are the possibilities? Be there for them to support their ideas and proposals, and help to facilitate the opportunity for them to become leaders for the team and the organization.

> **Tip:** Don't force anything. Let the team fulfill the space with their comments, suggestions or problems. Remember, that as Scrum Masters/Agile Coaches we are instruments that enable teams to get better results; so help them express their opinions freely. That will build the team's voice.

9) **Celebrate experimentation, it brings winning or learning**. At this stage of the team's development, people will be getting to know each other to understand who does what and how. Given that, people will try things to test the team's limits and to find their place within the group, and that's great. Celebrate those moments; when people make suggestions or bring ideas for improvement. Open a discussion and help the team to listen to the proposals. When people experiment, there are two potential outcomes: getting what you were expecting or learning something new. In both cases, there is learning for the team, and that knowledge becomes what makes the team resilient in the future. It will allow growing and willingness to try new things; it will battle fear and mitigate anxiety and make the team stronger over time.

    a. **How to do it?** Our role here is to connect on those moments. I like to take notes to register my observations during the day and use that as input to help me to prepare and select the topics that will be more appropriate to discuss within the retrospective agenda.

10) **Learn about the team**.
   a. **Timing:** It's really important that you learn when it is the best time to say something to the team. Timing matters! When it refers to working in groups, it could elevate or destroy the relationship between you and them. It unites or separates people, so please be patient when observing team dynamics, and how people relate to each other. Retrospectives are great for that.
   b. **Tone:** Using an appropriate voice tone is crucial when approaching the team, so invest the time to learn what tone fits better for each specific occasion and person in the team. Again, retrospectives are amazing for this.
   c. **Personalities & motivation:** I like to take the time with each team member so I can get to know each one and also, for each one to get to know me; building a better interpersonal relationship. I would do that by meeting one on one; during lunch time or even outside of the organization if needed, as a way to get ready for the iteration retrospective. You will be surprised about how much insight you will get from getting closer to each team member and learning who they are.

What type of activities would I recommend for iteration retrospectives when forming an agile team?

I've found there are some exercises that are particularly useful in iteration retrospectives when forming agile teams. These activities have been really helpful to facilitate my work with the teams during the forming stage; by offering some kind of structure to what the team needs to accomplish before moving to the next stage of the development process:

1) **Personal Stories**[37]
2) **How do we work here map**
3) **Agile at glance**
4) **Team's Identity**
5) **Expectations**

---

[37] For more details go to the "Tools and Exercise section" of the workbook

9. Iteration Report

An iteration report is a consolidated two page report that summarizes all the activity of the team during a particular iteration. Some of the elements considered within this report are:

- Project Status (Optional)
- Sprint Status
- Progress (Includes Product Backlog Items progression and issues that occurred during the iteration)
- Risks status found within the iteration.

When is the best moment to share the iteration report?

In order to use its content appropriately, I prefer to create the iteration report by the end of the iteration and share it with the team and the organization once the iteration retrospective is done and before the next iteration is over.

What's the goal of the iteration report?

The main goal of the iteration report is transparency to the organization of everything that the team has accomplished during the iteration. It's a tool to help the Scrum Master/Agile Coach support the team's progression, by collecting some historical data that could be useful when forming an agile team.

Who makes the iteration report?

The iteration report is created and distributed by the Scrum Master/Agile Coach at the end of iteration.

How is the iteration report created?

The iteration report is created by using information already gathered in previous steps of the iteration; especially the data gathered using the iteration review template at the iteration review meeting. Here are the suggested steps and how I do it:

Iteration Report Template – Overview – Part 1

Suggested Steps	
Purpose	**Techniques**

STEP 1 – Gather Project Status (Optional)

If project progress is tracked and project information is available at the team level, the goal here is to gather that information and make it available through the iteration report.	• Invite the Product Owner to fulfill this section of the iteration report by providing:
	
	   ○ **Project Name**
	
	   ○ **Start Date**
	
	   ○ **Estimated End Date (if available)**
	
	   ○ **Status:**
	
	      ▪ **On track:** Project has progressed according to original estimation and it will be released on schedule.
	
	      ▪ **Back on track:** Project hasn't achieved what was planned originally but it will be released on schedule.
	
	      ▪ **Off track:** Project is late and it won't be released on schedule.
	
	Note: if multiple projects then add a new row per project to the iteration report.

STEP 2 – Gather Iteration Status

Gather iteration status from what the team has shared during the iteration review	• I take photos of what the team has shared at the iteration review and then use gathered data to complete this section of the iteration report. (Iteration Review Template content)
	
	• The data gathered is used to completing the following fields in the iteration report:
	
	   ○ **Iteration Name**
	
	   ○ **Iteration Goal**

	o **Iteration Start/End Date**
	o **Items Forecast:** Sum/Count of Product Backlog Items forecast at the beginning of the iteration in story points/amount.
	o **Items Completed:** Sum/Count of Product Backlog Items completed by the end of the iteration in story points/amount.
	o **# Of Interruptions:** Count of unplanned Product Backlog Items added to the iteration backlog within the iteration.

STEP 3 – Gather Progress achieved by the end of the iteration

Identify Product Backlog items progress status and issues that impacted the team during the iteration	• From the iteration review template completed during the iteration review, take items gathered within the column "Things to demo" and "Updates" and write them down in this section of the report. • To complete the "Issues occurred during the iteration" section, I use the notes that I've collected during the iteration. In order to do that regularly, I use "Sticky notes" which I keep open in my computer to note things that interrupted or created an impact on the team's regular performance during the iteration.

STEP 4 – Assess Risks

Identify potential risks and assess impact on the team	• Using the notes gathered during the iteration, and after validating with the agile team, I would list the top two (2) risks and assess their impact on the team.
	 • To assess risks I use the following framework based on two measures, Impact and Likelihood:
	     o **Impact:** the extent to which the risk may affect the team and includes financial, reputational, employee, customer and operational impacts. There are three (3) main values to evaluate risk impact: Low, Medium, and High.
	     o **Likelihood:** the possibility it will occur and it can be represented in a qualitative or quantitative manner. There are three (3) main values to evaluate risk likelihood: Low, Medium, and High.

	o **Risk Response**: after the assessment has been completed, it's then up to the team to decide how they want to proceed with the information that was gathered. There are four (4) main responses that accompany risk:
	  ▪ Accept Risk
	  ▪ Mitigate Risk
	  ▪ Avoid Risk
	  ▪ Transfer Risk

Figure 62- Iteration report template - overview (Summary)

Iteration Report Template (Summary)

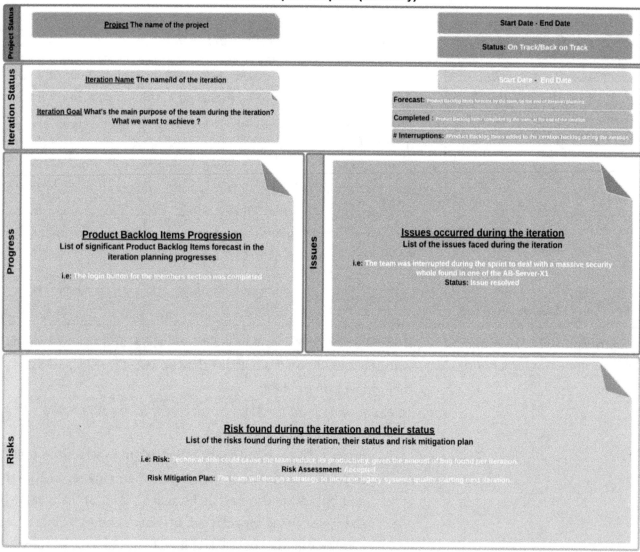

Figure 63- Iteration Report Template (Summary)

Iteration Report Template – Overview – Part 2 (Optional)

Charts

Suggested Steps	
Purpose	**Techniques**
STEP 1 – Team's Velocity Trend Chart	

Calculate and trend the team's velocity per Iteration	• Use *iteration review template* [38]*"Iteration status" column* content to register a trend chart in the fields that follow:
	
	   ○ **Items Forecast:** Sum of forecast product backlog items at the beginning of the iteration.
	
	   ○ **Items Completed:** Sum of completed product backlog items in story points by the end of the iteration.
	
	   ○ **# Of Interruptions (Added items):** Amount of items added to the iteration backlog. (Count).
	
	• Use the **Team's Performance report excel sheet calculator template**[39], to help you create **Team's Velocity Trend Chart** for the iteration that has completed.
	
	• Copy and paste the **Team's Velocity Trend Chart** created above in the corresponding box within the **iteration report template**[40].
	
	• Save a copy of the **iteration report template** file for future use.

STEP 2 – Team's Throughput Trend Chart	

Calculate and trend the team's throughput per iteration	• Use *iteration review template* "Iteration status" column content to register a trend chart in the fields that follow:
	
	   ○ **# Of Items Completed:** count of completed Product Backlog Items at the beginning of the iteration.
	
	   ○ **Items Completed:** sum of completed Product Backlog

---

[38] Jesus Mendez, "Iteration Review template", http://www.jesusmendez.ca/wp-content/uploads/2015/10/Jesuss-Sprint-Review-Template-V2.pdf

[39] Jesus Mendez, "Team's Performance report –ms-excel sheet template", http://www.jesusmendez.ca/wp-content/uploads/2016/01/Teams_Performance_report_excel_sheet-Forming-Agile-Teams.xlsx

[40] Jesus Mendez, Iteration report – ms-word template, http://www.jesusmendez.ca/wp-content/uploads/2016/01/Iteration_Report_ms-word_template_Forming-Agile-Teams.docx

Items by the end of the iteration in story points.

- o **# Of Interruptions (Added items):** count of unplanned Product Backlog Items added to the iteration backlog during the iteration.

- *Use the **Team's Performance report excel sheet template**[41], to help you create **Team's Throughput Trend Chart** for the iteration that has just completed.*

- *Copy and paste the **Team's Throughput Trend Chart** created above in the corresponding box within the **iteration report ms-word template**.*

- *Save the copy of the **iteration report ms-word template** file created above for future use.*

STEP 3 – Team's Performance Satisfaction Score Trend

Calculate and trend the team's performance satisfaction per iteration and profile	- *Use **Team's Performance Satisfaction template** content to register a trend chart in the fields that follow:*
	
	  o **# Of Items Completed:** count of completed Product Backlog Items at the beginning of the iteration.
	
	  o **Items Completed:** sum of completed Product Backlog Items by the end of the iteration in story points.
	
	  o **# Of Interruptions (Added items):** count of unplanned Product Backlog Items added to the iteration backlog during the iteration.
	
	 - *Use the **Team's Performance Satisfaction report excel sheet template**, to help you create **Team's Performance Satisfaction Score Trend Chart** for the iteration that has just completed.*

---

[41] Jesus Mendez, "Team's Performance report –ms-excel sheet template", http://www.jesusmendez.ca/wp-content/uploads/2016/01/Teams_Performance_report_excel_sheet-Forming-Agile-Teams.xlsx

	• Copy and paste the **Team's Performance Satisfaction Score Trend Chart** created above in the corresponding box within the iteration report ms-word template[42]. • Save the copy of the **iteration report ms-word template** file created above for future use.
STEP 4 – Comments	
Share some thoughts, reflections and opinions about the content of the trend charts.	• The Scrum Master/Agile Coach of the agile team gives you permission to share your opinion and interpretation of how the team is doing. I would keep it simple and to the point as much as possible.
STEP 5 – Make It Available	
Share iteration report with the agile team and the rest of the organization.	• Explain to the agile team that reporting the status of the iteration is part of your responsibilities. Given so, let them know that you're about to share a summary of what the team has accomplished. You will be sharing with the team and some other people within the organization. • Once you get a go signal, I like to share the iteration report first with the agile team, and ask them if I missed anything by sending them an email with the report attached. • I do not wait any longer than ten (10) minutes for feedback and then I send the report out to the rest of the organization.

Figure 64- Iteration report template - overview (Charts)

---

[42] Jesus Mendez, Iteration report – ms-word template, http://www.jesusmendez.ca/wp-content/uploads/2016/01/Iteration_Report_ms-word_template_Forming-Agile-Teams.docx

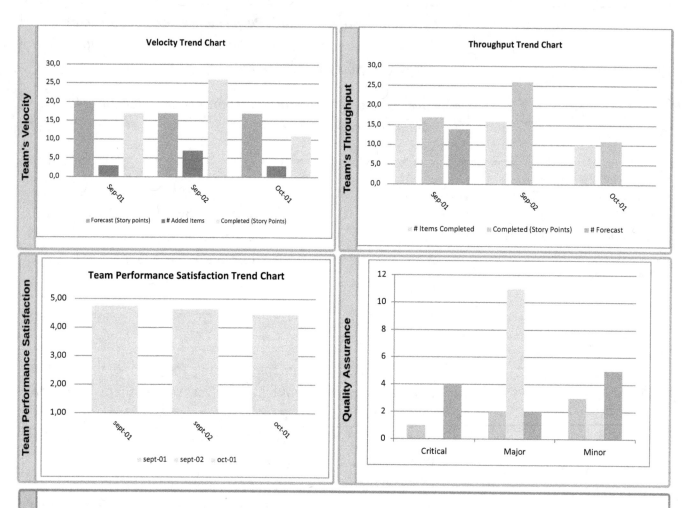

Figure 65-Iteration Report Template - Charts

Lorem ipsum dolor sit amet, consectetur adipiscing elit. Etiam et tortor consequat, vestibulum tortor in, iaculis elit. Aliquam egestas porta condimentum. Nulla scelerisque egestas eros, id tempor sem convallis sed. Maecenas ultrices libero sapien, eu aliquet elit consectetur quis. Pellentesque consectetur erat sed elit pharetra condimentum. Morbi sodales libero ut neque vestibulum bibendum.
accumsan. Duis luctus nisl nisl, sed rhoncus felis tincidunt quis.

Final Thoughts

Congratulations! You have bravely navigated through the nine (9) steps of forming agile teams for the first time and hopefully I have inspired you to do great things with your agile team. But now what? What's the next step in the team's journey?

Here some ideas to help you to continue the incredible journey that you have started one hundred and eight (108) pages ago:

- Continue iterating through the forming stage of the team's development process until some of the signs that follow, are visible within the team:

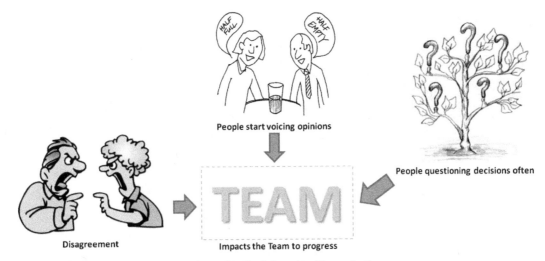

Figure 66- Final thoughts (Now what)

- Keep experimenting and trying to improve on the things that work for the team/organization in the first place.
- Allow yourself to continue exploring this path of self-growth and be gentle when doing so, especially with you.
- Get ready to be surprised, try to enjoy it and be compassionate with others especially with yourself.
- Give yourself 100% every single day, no matter how hard it seems; you are doing the most beautiful job in the world, which is helping others to help themselves.
- Be your most authentic self, that's the most beautiful gift that you already have.
- Enjoy the ride, smiling and sharing each moment with the people around you and do it with passion and love.

Tools and Exercises

In this section we provide you with step by step instructions to use the tools and exercises mentioned in the "Iteration retrospective" section of the book.

Iteration Retrospective Agenda Template

Summary

- **Date:** Date of the iteration retrospective.
- **Status:** To do/Doing/Done.
- **Expected Duration:** X hour(s), Real duration: Y hours and Z minutes.
- **Facilitator:** Name of the facilitator.
- **Intentions:** i.e. my intentions today are to help us explore the team reactions when facing some fears that were exposed during the iteration and find ways to deal with them.
- **Retrospective Goal(s):** i.e. help us face fear and do it without distraction.

Participants

List of iteration retrospective participants

- <Team member names> + <Product Owner name>

Agenda

List of iteration retrospective proposed activities

1) **Set the stage** – activity: i.e. check-in question - how do you feel right now?
2) **Generate Insights** – activity: i.e. let's draw and share the story of the iteration with pictures.
3) **Gather data** – activity: i.e. what is common between each individual story? What is curious about those common factors? What do you think are the positive elements? In your opinion, which aspects, in our control, could be improved? What possibilities do we have to make things better?
4) **Decide what to do** – activity: i.e. Open list (What, Who, By When).
5) **Close retrospective** – activity: i.e. Retro dart (I spoke openly?).

Notes: Additional notes/observations/take-away gathered during the iteration retrospective.

Team Backlog Action Items

List of action items decided by the team during the iteration retrospective.

Personal Stories

Purpose of the exercise: Get to know each other better (Building trust).

Time required: From one (1) hour to one and a half (1.5) hours maximum.

Pre-requisites: Post-its, markers, a table, **storytelling cards**[43] or some pictures printed from internet, a facilitator.

Preparation: 10 – 30 minutes to print out the required material and setup the room. Spread cards on the table; write the name of each participant and stick it on a specific place on one of the walls of the room. Create/reuse the weather report on a flip chart.

How many participants: Minimum three, maximum to be determined.

Recommended: This activity is recommended to be done with new teams, or when new team members join an existing team.

Iteration Retrospective proposed agenda
1) Set the stage - **Weather report**[44] from the book **Agile retrospectives: making good teams great**[45]
2) Gather data - Let's share a Personal Story
3) Generate insights - Learning and possibilities
4) Decide what to do - Take action
5) Close retrospective – Evaluate the **Team's performance satisfaction template**[46] during the iteration retrospective.

Instructions
1) Set the stage – Weather report (10 minutes)

Welcome participants to the iteration retrospective and once everyone is in, present your proposed agenda, previously created. Once you have finished, ask the following question "Is there any other subject that you would prefer to discuss instead?" And wait for

---

[43] Management 3.0, Story telling cards, https://management30.com/wp-content/uploads/2015/03/Improv-Cards-Letter-CJA-v1.00.pdf
[44] Plan for Retrospectives, "Weather report", http://www.plans-for-retrospectives.com/?id=2
[45] Esther Derby, Agile retrospectives: making good teams great, http://www.amazon.com/Agile-Retrospectives-Making-Teams-Great/dp/0977616649/
[46] Jesus Mendez, Team's performance satisfaction template, http://www.jesusmendez.ca/wp-content/uploads/2015/10/Jesuss-Team's-Performance-Satisfaction-Template-V2.1.pdf

answers. If somebody proposes a topic, ask the team what they want to do? And follow whatever they want. If the team chooses your proposed agenda then go to the next step. If they don't, then skip this exercise and facilitate the 'new' conversation without any regrets.

- Invite them to do a **weather check**[47], and then share, individually, how they feel. I like to use post-its and ask each team member to write down their name and include their weather check with it.
- Be curious and ask them "Who is willing to share the reasons behind your choice of the weather check report? Be silent and wait at least 30 seconds before saying anything. Remember it is their meeting, so be patient and wait. Let them talk, listening to all the answers. Once each person has finished sharing, be sure to thank them.

2) Let's share a Personal Story (20 to 30 minutes)

Explain that most of the team effort during the forming stage is going to be focused on building the relationship of trust. Given that, we are going to play "Personal Stories". Here are the steps for this activity:

- Spread **storytelling cards**[48] on the table. Make each one visible to be chosen.
- Ask participants to think about a personal story, something that nobody in the team knows about them.
- Invite participants to pick at least three (3) cards from the table and then build their personal story from them.
- Invite participants to go to the pre-selected area in the room with their name on it and then stick their cards to the wall to share their personal story. Give the team three (3) minutes to build their personal story.

    Special note: I like to participate in this activity, in order to share my own personal story with the team to help build the relationship of trust too, but that is optional.

- Ask who wants to share their personal story first. Then ask who is next? Repeat this step until everyone has shared their personal story.

---

[37] Plan for Retrospectives, "Weather check", http://www.plans-for-retrospectives.com/?id=2
[48] Management 3.0, "Story telling cards", https://management30.com/wp-content/uploads/2015/03/Improv-Cards-Letter-CJA-v1.00.pdf

- Invite the team to discuss what we have learned about our colleagues? In the meantime, take notes about what the team has told you they learned.

3) Learning and possibilities (20 minutes)

Explore together the following question: what do you think is possible when we trust each other? Give the team one (1) minute to think and then invite them to share their thoughts in pairs and list at least two possibilities, one per post-it. Give the team three (3) minutes to do that.

- Ask the team to stick the possibilities they created on the wall and then to choose the team's favorite one; give them three votes per person. They can use the votes in any way they want.

4) Take action (20 minutes)

Invite them reflect in pairs about the following question: what action could the team do to make that possibility become a reality, starting next iteration? Give them three (3) to five (5) minutes. Each group should suggest at least one action item to share.

- Invite each group to stick their actions on the wall. Help the team to group them into categories. Ask each group to stick their actions on the wall.
    i. Help the team to group them in categories.
    ii. Invite the team to decide what to do for the next iteration, who is responsible and when will the action item be completed.

5) Close retrospective - Team's performance satisfaction template (5 minutes)

Close retrospective by thanking them for their active participation and invite them to evaluate their level of the team's performance satisfaction during the retrospective using the **Team's performance satisfaction template**[49].

Expected outcome
- The team gets to know team members from another perspective.
- Make people vulnerable by sharing personal stories with their colleagues.
- Teach the team that being vulnerable in front of others can be fun and highly interesting.

---

[49] Jesus Mendez, "Team's performance satisfaction template", http://www.jesusmendez.ca/wp-content/uploads/2015/10/Jesuss-Team's-Performance-Satisfaction-Template-V2.1.pdf

- Create possibilities and new connections between team members.
- Build the relationship of trust within the team.
- Have fun.

How do we work map
The Team teaching the Scrum Master/Agile Coach

Purpose of the exercise: Discover how things are done within the team and more.

Time required: Forty five (45) minutes to one (1) hour maximum.

Pre-requisites: Post-its, markers, an empty wall, a facilitator.

Preparation: 20 minutes to print out the required material and create the **Temperature reading**[50] and the **Feedback Door – Smiles**[51] flip charts.

How many participants: Minimum one, maximum to be determined.

Recommended: This activity is recommended when starting to work with a new team where you are going to be the Scrum Master/Agile Coach.

Iteration Retrospective proposed agenda
1) Set the stage - **Temperature reading**
2) Gather data - Let's teach our Scrum Master/Agile Coach how the team works.
3) Generate insights - Let's map our development process with the agile framework in use.
4) Decide what to do - Top two (2) things that could be improved.
5) Close retrospective - **Feedback Door – Smiles by Boeffi**[52]

Instructions

1) Set the stage – Temperature reading (10 minutes)

Welcome participants to the iteration retrospective and once everyone is in, present your proposed agenda, previously created. Once you have finished, ask the following question "Is there any other subject that you would prefer to discuss instead?" And wait for answers. If somebody proposes a topic, ask the team what they want to do? And follow whatever they want. If the team chooses your proposed agenda then go to the next step.

[50] Plan for retrospectives, "Temperature reading", http://plans-for-retrospectives.com/?id=22
[51] Plan for retrospectives, "Feedback Door - Smiles", http://plans-for-retrospectives.com/?id=23
[52] Boeffi, "Feedback Door – Smiles", http://boeffi.net/tutorials/roti-return-on-time-invested-wie-funktionierts/

If they don't then skip this exercise and facilitate the 'new' conversation without any regrets.

- Now is time to check our individual temperature, in order to acknowledge how everyone feels before the retrospective starts.
- Ask participants to write their name on a post-it note and voluntarily stick it to the temperature reading flip chart, in the most convenient place which represents their current temperature.
- Once everyone in the room has done it, invite participants to take a look at it and be curious about the results. Acknowledge the fact that everyone is different and we should respect that.
- Thank the participants for sharing and for their openness.

2) Let's teach our Scrum Master/Agile Coach how the team works (20 to 30 minutes)

Invite the team to teach you about the work the team does. In order to do that, I like to draw on a white board a starting point at the left and from there ask the team to guide you through the workflow.

- Invite the Product Owner to tell you how an organization requirement gets into the team's workflow.
- From there draw a starting point for the team's workflow.
- Ask questions about each step of the process, and repeat what the team is saying, to be sure that nothing gets lost.
- Listen carefully to what the team is saying and repeat the previous step until the team asks you to stop.
- Be sure that you have covered everything.

3) Let's map our development process with the agile framework in use (20 minutes)

Now invite the team to teach you about their agile framework: Kanban, Scrum, XP, Crystal, Safe, Open Agile, etc.

- Ask the team to navigate you through the agile framework that's in use.
- Invite them to map their workflow with the agile framework in use:
  - i. i.e.: Planning how to consistently develop a requirement that happens during sprint planning.
  - ii. Be curious and ask open ended questions to understand it.
- Repeat previous step until all steps are mapped with the agile framework in use.

- Take a picture of the resultant diagram for future reference.

4) Top two (2) things that could be improved.

In pairs or threesomes, invite the team to invest ten (10) minutes to identify two (2) things that require improvement in their development process and ask them to use post-it notes to write them down.

- Invite each group to present its ideas to the rest of the team, by describing:
    - i. What needs to be improved
    - ii. For what reason
- Repeat previous step until all groups have shared their ideas.
- Invite the team to organize in priority all their ideas for improvement. Give the team all the time they need to do this.
- Take a picture of the prioritized improvement list.

5) Close retrospective – Feedback Door – Smiles (5 minutes)

Close the retrospective by thanking everyone for the team's hard work and then invite them for closure by giving you feedback at the 'Feedback Door – Smiles' flip chart. It's up to you to ask for anonymous or non-anonymous feedback.

Expected outcome

- Shared understanding of the team's development process.
- Team's alignment about what's working and what needs to be improved.
- Empower the team to own their development process.
- Install habit of continuous improvement through retrospectives.
- Get to know each other better.
- Build the relationship of trust between the new team and you as their Scrum Master/Agile Coach.

Agile at glance

Purpose of the exercise: The goal of this retrospective is to start the conversation within the team about the team's development process, in this case, by using the Agile-Scrum framework. By asking open ended questions, the facilitator will help the team discover the areas of improvement identified by the team, help with clarifying some concepts and show the team how easy it is to inspect and adapt their own development process.

Pre-requisites: Agile-Scrum at a Glance – Baseline[53] for Scrum teams or an image from the internet of the agile framework used by the team, a facilitator, a board, some markers, some post-its and a good attitude.

Preparation: 20 minutes to print out the required material, write on the board four bubbles and the four agile values for them (using the Agile Values Cheers Up exercises references below) and create the **Retro dart**[54] flip chart.

How many participants: minimum one, maximum to be determined.

Time required: Between fifty (50) minutes and one (1) hour, depending on how engaged the team is when discussing improvements.

Recommended: This activity can be used with new teams (everybody is new), when a new member is joining the scrum team or even when the Scrum Master/Agile Coach/Facilitator is the one joining the team. The main focus of the activity is to get alignment about the Scrum framework, which could be used to guiding the Scrum Master/Agile Coach/Facilitator with:
- What needs to be improved and in which order (priority)?
- What is not clear/unknown about the scrum framework? (What requires reinforcement?)
- What's working and what's not?

---

[53] Jesus Mendez, "Agile-Scrum at a glance – baseline", http://tastycupcakes.org/wp-content/uploads/2015/07/Agile-Scrum-At-Glance-Baseline.pdf
[54] Plan for retrospectives, "Retro Dart", http://plans-for-retrospectives.com/?id=83

Iteration Retrospective proposed agenda

1) Set the stage – **Agile Values Cheers Up**[55] by Jesus Mendez
2) Gather data – Agile Scrum at a Glance -> Explore and identify
3) Generate insights – Agile Scrum at a Glance -> Discuss
4) Decide what to do – Agile Scrum at a Glance -> Group and decide
5) Close retrospective – **Retro dart**[56] by **Philipp Flenker**[57]

Instructions

1) Set the stage – Agile Values Cheers Up (15 to 20 minutes)

Welcome participants to the iteration retrospective and once everyone is in, present your proposed agenda, previously created. Once you have finished, ask the following question "Is there any other subject that you would prefer to discuss instead?" And wait for answers. If somebody proposes a topic, ask the team what they want to do? And follow whatever they want. If the team chooses your proposed agenda then go to the next step. If they don't then skip this exercise and facilitate the 'new' conversation without any regrets.

- Ask participants to write down instances when their colleagues have displayed one of the agile values.
  - o 1 cheerful sticky note per example.
- In turn, let everyone post their note in the corresponding bubble and read them out loud.
- Rejoice in how you embody agile core values.

2) Explore & identify (5 minutes)

- Share a copy of the **Agile–framework at a glance baseline image**[58] that you have printed out previously, with each participant.

---

[55] Plan for retrospectives, "Agile Values Cheers Up", http://plans-for-retrospectives.com/?id=90
[56] Plan for retrospectives, "Retro Dart", http://plans-for-retrospectives.com/?id=83
[57] Phillip Flenker, "Retro Dart", http://www.philippflenker.de/
[58] Agile for All," The Agile Scrum framework at a glance",
https://www.google.ca/search?q=agile+scrum+at+glance&rls=com.microsoft:en-US:%7Breferrer:source%3F%7D&rlz=1I7GGLL_en&source=lnms&tbm=isch&sa=X&ved=0ahUKEwj90YKn24DNAhUPxCYKHY_aDgsQ_AUIBygB&biw=1366&bih=643#imgrc=OrsVBpuY5UVQYM%3A

- Ask the team to take a look at the "Agile –framework at a glance baseline image" and ask them to write down one issue per post-it, about those areas in the chart that: (1) Require some kind of improvement (2) Are not clear/unknown.
- Note: it's up to the facilitator to limit the amount of reported issues, so you can reach the time frame that works best for you.
- Set a time frame between three (3) to five (5) minutes, and then let the team alone write down the issues found.
- Once the time frame is reached, ask the team if anybody needs more time. If the answer is no, then move on to the next step.

3) Discuss (30 minutes)

- Open the floor to discussion by asking for volunteers to expose identified issues.
- At this point of the activity, it's suggested to ask open ended questions in order to clarify each identified issue. Questions such as:
  - What is important about the issue that you are presenting to us?
  - What have you considered when raising the issue?
- Once everybody has presented their own issue, it's time to move on to the next step.

4) Group and decide (15 to 20 minutes)

- Now that everything has been discussed, ask for a volunteer to help the team with grouping all the post-its, by using the areas available in the "Agile – framework at a glance baseline image".
- Give the team some dot stickers to vote (usually I will give each team member 1 vote).
- Once everybody has dot voted, ask them to organize the identified issues in order, based on how many dot votes each issue received.
- Now ask the team to identify one action that will help the team with improving each identified issue.
- **Note:** If something is not clear/unknown it is up to you to decide when to explain it. Although, I usually do it once the question is raised.

5) Close retrospective – Retro dart (5 minutes)

- Close the retrospective by thanking everyone for their hard work during the session.
- Invite the team to answer the three questions asked in the Retro dart flip chart posted on the door at the entrance to the room before leaving, by sticking their name and answers, one per post it, on each of the three questions.

Expected outcome

- Common and shared understanding about where the team is regarding the agile framework.
- Things that are considered important about the team's development process are shared.
- The team is empowered to adapt its own development process to its own needs.
- A high level actionable improvement plan has been created by the team.
- The first seed for a self-organized team has been deployed.

Team's Identity
Our ideal team (characteristics, values and a name that is worthy)

Purpose of the exercise: The goal of the retrospective is to help the team with building its identity, setting shared values and creating a name to tie everything together.

Pre-requisites: a facilitator, a board, some markers, some post-its, a set of **storytelling cards**[59], a case of beer or a bottle of wine and a good attitude.

Preparation: 10 minutes to set the room properly.

How many participants: minimum three people, maximum to be determined.

Time required: from one and a half (1.5) hours to two (2) hours.

---

[59] Management 3.0, "Story telling cards", https://management30.com/wp-content/uploads/2015/03/Improv-Cards-Letter-CJA-v1.00.pdf

Recommended: I would recommend that this retrospective be done, once the team's development process has been discussed, the workflow has been mapped and the team has been working together using an agile framework for at least two (2) months.

Iteration Retrospective proposed agenda

1) Set the stage – What's awesome about my team by Jesus Mendez
2) Gather data – Picturing my ideal team
3) Generate insights – Present and discuss
4) Decide what to do – Group and decide
5) Close retrospective – its beer/wine time!

Instructions

1) Set the stage – What's awesome about my team (10 – 15 minutes)?

Welcome participants to the iteration retrospective and once everyone is in, present your proposed agenda, previously created. Once you have finished, ask the following question "Is there any other subject that you would prefer to discuss instead?" And wait for answers. If somebody proposes a topic, ask the team what they want to do? And follow whatever they want. If the team chooses your proposed agenda then go to the next step. If they don't then skip this exercise and facilitate the 'new' conversation without any regrets.

- Share a white piece of paper with participants. One each.
  - o Invite them to write down the following text on it, covering all the empty space:
    - ▪ What's awesome about my team is _____
      And that makes me feel _____
  - o In two (2) minutes ask them to fill out the empty lines and then wait until everyone is done.
- Ask for a volunteer to read their paper sheet out loud.
- Invite the team to celebrate by cheering or applauding.
- Ask participant to stick the paper sheet on the wall titled "What's awesome about my team".
- In turn, invite others to repeat the two previous steps until the whole team has done it.

- Invite the team to be curious and ask questions about what the others have shared in their paper sheets until there are no more questions.

2) Picturing my ideal team (20 to 30 minutes)

- Invite team members to select from the table one storytelling card that represents the image of the ideal team.
- Now in a big post-it (4x4), ask them to write down the top five values of that ideal team. To inspire them, search in Google the following phrase "Team values list".
- Ask participants to write down a name for that ideal team.
- Invite participants to choose a wall in the room to stick its selected picture and the list of team values.

3) Present & discuss (30 to 40 minutes)

- Invite participants to present to the rest of the team, its selected picture, the list of team values of its ideal team and the ideal name that comes with it.
- Ensure that all participants share their ideas with the rest of the team.
- Ask participants to form pairs or threesomes to talk about their ideal team.
- Invite them to join all group pictures and create their ideal team.
- Take individual team values list to create a group of the top five (5) team values list.
- From the ideal team names, ask the group to choose their favorite name.

4) Group and decide (15 to 20 minutes)

- Now ask the groups to voluntarily present their ideal team, its values and its ideal name.
- Repeat previous step until all groups have presented its ideal team.
- Ask groups to form one team and join the pictures to form their ideal team, choose the top five values of that team from the lists previously created.
- Give team members some dots stickers (three each) to vote for the name of the team.
- Now ask for a volunteer to present the pictures (characteristics) of the ideal team, the list of values that the team is aiming for and the chosen name for it.
- Celebrate that the team has a new name!

- Take some pictures of the activity to keep names at hand if, in any case, the team decides to change it later.
- Document it all (an email is good enough) and share it with the team.

5) Close retrospective- It's beer/wine time (5-10 minutes)

- Close the retrospective by thanking everyone for their hard work during the session.
- Invite the team to celebrate by sharing a glass of beer/wine and enjoy.

Expected outcome

- Common and shared understanding about what the team's vision of itself is.
- The team has created an entity that's tangible and it has a name. This will help with leading team actions and behaviors in the future.
- A lot of fun, sharing and laughing.

Expectations
Let's make it visible

Purpose of the exercise: The goal of this retrospective is to increase the trust in the room by sharing expectations within the team. It's a way to get a better understanding of what teammates are willing to offer and what everybody expects from everybody else.

Pre-requisites: a facilitator, a board, some markers, a copy of the expectation paper sheet per participant and a good attitude.

Preparation: 5-10 minutes to make a copy per participant of the expectation paper sheet.

How many participants: minimum two, maximum to be determined.

Time required: Between forty five (45) minutes and one (1) hour, depending on how engaged the team is when discussing expectations.

Recommended: This activity could be used with new teams (everybody is new), when a new member is joining the scrum team or even when the Scrum Master/Agile Coach/Facilitator is the one joining the team. To maximize outcome, I personally prefer to run this retrospective when the team has already done at least three (3) or four (4) retrospectives together.

Iteration Retrospective proposed agenda

1) Set the stage – **Appreciations**[60] from the book **Agile Retrospectives: making good teams great**[61] taken from 'The Satire Model: Family Therapy and Beyond'
2) Gather data – **Expectations**[62] by **Valerie Santillo**[63]
3) Generate insights – Let's review our expectation paper sheets and share
4) Decide what to do – The one thing that I can improve
5) Close retrospective – **Please and Surprised**[64] by Unknown

Instructions

1) Set the stage – Appreciations (10 to 15 minutes)
Welcome participants to the iteration retrospective and once everyone is in, present your proposed agenda, previously created. Once you have finished, ask the following question "Is there any other subject that you would prefer to discuss instead?" And wait for answers. If someone proposes a topic, ask the team what they want to do? And follow whatever they want. If the team chooses your proposed agenda then go to the next step. If they don't then skip this exercise and facilitate the 'new' conversation without any regrets.

- Now it's time for some appreciations.
- Invite participants to appreciate what the others did for them or the team during the iteration and say it out loud.
- Start saying: I appreciate that <Team member name> did <thing> during the iteration. Thank you for that.
- Continue until all participants have done their round and no one speaks for at least 1 minute.

---

[60] Plan for retrospectives, "Appreciations", http://plans-for-retrospectives.com/?id=15
[61] Esther Derby, Agile retrospectives: making good teams great, http://www.amazon.com/Agile-Retrospectives-Making-Teams-Great/dp/0977616649/
[62] Plan for retrospectives, "Expectations", http://plans-for-retrospectives.com/?id=62
[63] Valerie Santillo, "Expectations", http://agileyammering.com/2013/01/25/expectations/
[64] Plan for retrospectives, "Please and Surprised", http://plans-for-retrospectives.com/?id=45

2) Expectations (20 minutes)

- Share a copy of the Expectations paper sheet that you have completed with each participant present in the room.
- Invite participants to fill out the top half of the Expectation paper sheet for themselves by answering the following questions:
  - What my teammates can expect from me
  - What I expect from my teammates
- When everyone is finished, they pass their paper to the left and start reviewing the sheet that was passed to them.
- In the lower half they write what they personally expect from that person, sign it and pass it on.

3) Discuss (15 minutes)

- Invite participants to take a minute to read carefully what has been written on their expectation paper sheet.
- Open the discussion by asking for volunteers to reveal their findings.
- At this point of the retrospective, it's suggested to ask open ended questions in order to enable communication between team members.
- Observe participants and their behavior. Sometimes people face unexpected things within the exercise.
- Once silence has invaded the room, it's time to move on to the next step.

4) One individual thing that I can improve (10 to 15 minutes)

- Now that everything has been discussed, invite participants to take a moment to reflect about one thing that they consider individually could be improved.
- Tell participants to feel free to share or not share their finding with the team.
- Allow everyone to take a moment to digest the exercise and take all comments and suggestions as gifts given by their colleagues, so they can learn from it.

5) Close retrospective (5 minutes)

- Close the retrospective by thanking everyone for being so open and showing some vulnerability to help the team improve.

- Invite the team to make a quick go-round of the room and let each participant point out one finding of the retrospective that either surprised or pleased them (or both).

Expected outcome

- Expectations within the team are shared.
- Enables the team to get to know each other in a deeper way.
- First team exposure to potential judgement and direct feedback.

Glossary

:: A

Accept Risk: the cost to mitigate is higher than the cost to bear the risk, so you move forward.

Avoid Risk: an even of high likelihood and significant financial impact, so take a pro-active stance.

:: B

Backlog: An inventory of Agile stories/tasks/items that can be been selected to be worked on.

Bug: a behavior/layout problem that goes against functional specifications and/or approved design that provides business value. [Needs to be addressed, but can choose when].

:: D

Definition of Done (DOD): a set of checkpoints agreed upon by a Scrum team to determine the completion of tasks.

Development Team: the role within an agile Team accountable for managing, organizing and doing all development work required to create a releasable Increment of the product per iteration.

:: F

Forecast (of functionality): the selection of items from the Product Backlog a Development team deems feasible for implementation per Iteration.

:: I

Impact (Risk): the extent the risk may affect the company and includes financial, reputation, employee, customer and operational impacts.

Impediment: Anything that creates any sort of perceived resistance, friction or drag on the project. That friction can manifest as personal conflicts, slow software network problems or even technical debt. All these problems can slow down a team's progress.

Iteration: time-boxed event of 30 days, or less, that serves as a container for the other iteration events and activities. Iterations are done consecutively, without intermediate gaps.

Iteration Backlog: an overview of the development work to realize the Iteration's goal, typically a forecast of functionality and the work needed to deliver that functionality.

Iteration Goal: a short expression of the purpose of Iteration, often a business problem that is addressed. Functionality might be adjusted during the Iteration in order to achieve the Iteration Goal.

:: L

Likelihood (Risk): the possibility it will occur and may be represented in a qualitative or quantitative manner.

Line Manager: the role within an organization accountable for guiding, coaching, supporting, evaluating and assisting team members in an agile organization.

:: M

Mitigate Risk: try to control the impact of the risk; allow it, but play constant attention to seek minimal exposure.

:: P

Product Backlog: an ordered list of the work to be done in order to create, maintain and sustain a product.

Product Owner: the role accountable for maximizing the value of a product, primarily by incrementally managing and expressing business and functional expectations for a product to the Development Team(s).

:: R

Risk: a situation involving exposure to damage, harm or loss.

:: S

Scrum: a framework to support teams in complex product development. Scrum consists of Scrum Teams and their associated roles, events, artifacts, and rules, as defined in the Scrum Guide TM.

Scrum Master: the role within an Agile Team (Especially in Scrum Teams) accountable for guiding, coaching, teaching and assisting a Scrum Team and its environments in a proper understanding and use of Scrum.

Stakeholder: a person external to the Agile Team with a specific interest in and knowledge of a product that is required for incremental discovery. Represented by the Product Owner and actively engaged with the Agile Team at Iteration Review.

Stories: items that are created for an agile team to work on that have business value. They are based on customer wants and have validation criteria associated to them.

:: V

Velocity: an optional, but often used, indication of the average amount of Product Backlog turned into an Increment of product during the iteration by a Scrum Team, tracked by the Development Team for use within the Scrum Team.

Table of figures

Notes and references

Section: it's all done by Iterations

- From Agilealliance.org: Resource Guide, http://guide.agilealliance.org/guide/iteration.html
- Davies Rachel from AgileCoach.typead.com: Sprint vs. iteration, http://agilecoach.typead.com/agile-coaching/2014/02/sprint-vs-iteration.html
- The Planning Game from Shore James web site: The planning game, http://www.jamesshore.com/Agile-Book/the_planning_game.html
- Mike Cohn web site: Differences between scrum and extreme programming, https://www.mountaingoatsoftware.com/blog/differences-between-scrum-and-extreme-programming
- Deming Cycle, PCDA http://www.isixsigma.com/dictionary/deming-cycle-pdca
- From The Manifesto for Agile Software Development: Principles behind the manifesto, http://www.agilemanifesto.org/principles.html

Section 1: Planning the team transformation process

- Scott W Ambler in his article Active Stakeholder Participation: An Agile Best Practice. (2013). Retrieved September 04, 2015, from Agile Modeling: http://agilemodeling.com/essays/activeStakeholderParticipation.htm
- Stakeholder categories are from Carl Kessler and Sweitzer John book Outside-in Software Development, IBM Press, 2007
- Susan Johnston, "The Arc of a Coaching Conversation", Agile Coaching online course, 2014
- C. H Green, D. H Maister & R. M. Galford (2000). The Trusted Advisor. New York: Free Press

Section 5: Helping the team to stay focused

- Tom Perry, AgileTools website: Task boards telling a compelling agile story, https://agiletools.wordpress.com/2007/11/24/task-boards-telling-a-compelling-agile-story
- Tom Perry. The Little Book of Impediments http://leanpub.com/ImpedimentsBook
- Leanne Howard from the Planit.net.au web site: Identifying Dysfunction in an agile team, https://www.planit.net.au/resource/identifying-dysfunction-in-an-agile-team
- Patrick Lencioni, Overcoming the five dysfunctions of a team, a field guide for leaders, managers and facilitators

Section: Team's Product Road Map

- Roman Pichler Blog: 10 Tips for creating Agile Product Roadmaps, http://www.romanpichler.com/blog/10-tips-creating-agile-product-roadmap/

- Vikas Jain: Experiments with Agile Planning Levels,
https://www.scrumalliance.org/community/articles/2015/april/experiments-with-agile-planning-levels

Section 6: Iteration Product Backlog Refinement

- Mike Cohn web site: Product Backlog Refinement (Grooming),
https://www.mountaingoatsoftware.com/blog/product-backlog-refinement-grooming
- Product Backlog Refinement Meeting (Video), Scrumtrainingseries.com,
http://scrumtrainingseries.com/BacklogRefinementMeeting/BacklogRefinementMeeting.htm
- Roman Pichler, Grooming the Product Backlog, http://www.romanpichler.com/blog/grooming-the-product-backlog/

Section 8: Iteration Retrospective

- What's a retrospective? http://www.retrospectives.com
- Ben Linders. What's an Agile Retrospective and Why would you do it?,
http://www.benlinders.com/2013/whats-an-agile-retrospective-and-why-would-you-do-it
- Ben Linders & Luis Goncalves, Getting Value out of agile retrospectives.
- Kevin Cashman, The Pause Principle: Step back to lead forward.
- Corinna Baldauf, Retromat, Plan for Retrospectives. http://plans-for-retrospectives.com
- Jürgen Apello, Management 3.0. Improvisation cards,
https://management30.com/product/improv-cards/

Section 9: Iteration Report

- Risk Management concepts on this section inspired from Cathy Axais, my boss and Quality Assurance specialist at Seedbox Technologies Inc.

Stay in Touch

I'd love to hear about your journey and learn from your experiences. You can contact me at **www.jesusmendez.ca** where I'll be sharing ideas and best practices from Scrum Masters around the world. I invite you to join the team transformation conversation!

Via **twitter** I've created the hash tag **#TransformingTeams** to keep the conversation open. Also you can reach me directly by sending a message to **@chuzzete**.

Let's connect via email too and change the world together. Just **send me an email** to **transformingteams@jesusmendez.ca** and I'll be more than happy to connect and collaborate with you.

What's next

This workbook is part of our agile teams from forming to performing series. Be the first to hear about new publications, special offers, exclusive articles, news and more! Get on the list for our e-newsletter by going to **www.jesusmendez.ca**

We are grateful to the readers, authors and other friends who consider themselves part of the team transformation movement.

www.ingramcontent.com/pod-product-compliance
Lightning Source LLC
LaVergne TN
LVHW081757050326
832903LV00027B/1997